SPEECH & DRAMA DEPT.
ST. JOHN'S LAND
MORAY HOUSE COLLEGE OF EDUCATION

# THE THEATRE THROUGH THE AGES

THE
# THEATRE
THROUGH
# THE AGES

*by*

JAMES CLEAVER

*illustrated by*
*the author*

LONDON
GEORGE G. HARRAP AND COMPANY LTD.
SYDNEY TORONTO BOMBAY STOCKHOLM

TO

HELEN

*First published* 1946
*by* GEORGE G. HARRAP & CO. LTD.
182 High Holborn, London, W.C.1

*Reprinted February* 1948

THIS BOOK IS PRODUCED IN
COMPLETE CONFORMITY WITH THE
AUTHORIZED ECONOMY STANDARDS

*Made in Great Britain*
*Composed in Bembo type and printed by*
R. & R. CLARK, LIMITED, *Edinburgh*

*Lithographs drawn on the plate by the author and*
*printed by* JARROLD AND SONS, LTD., *Norwich*

# PREFACE

WITH THE GROWTH OF YOUTH ORGANIZATIONS throughout the country, and the possibility of part-time compulsory education up to the age of eighteen, interest is growing in dramatic performances as part of the scheme of education. The study of plays, particularly Shakespeare's, and the committing to memory of whole passages, have been the bane of many in their early school days. Too many people have been forced into a hearty dislike of Shakespeare and all the other dramatists the study of whose work comes in the school time-table under " English." But to bring a play to life on the stage is an entirely different matter. Not only is the play studied closely during rehearsals, but the performance often gives new point to the lines. And the many activities necessary in staging a play—the making of costumes, the building of scenery, the fixing of lights—besides developing talent, make for co-operation and team-work. And the important thing is that it is enjoyed by all.

If we have decided to produce a play, what shall we put on, and how shall it be done? From the past we have an extensive library of plays by the greatest English writers. Having chosen one at random, we must first read and understand it, and then decide how it shall be performed. To understand a play written in the past we must first understand the people of those times, the actors for whom it was written—for plays were usually written for certain actors—then the stage on which it was first performed, what scenery there was (if any), what effects accompanied the play, and, finally, what were the kinds of audiences who paid to see it. If we can reconstruct the conditions of the theatre for which the play was written, then we shall understand more fully its value as a work of art.

This book has been written as a short guide to these conditions in the past. It is by no means exhaustive—it could hardly be so in such small compass—but if it stimulates interest in the further study of stage, theatre, actors, and audiences it will have served its purpose.

The illustrations have been designed to supplement the text in giving as much information as possible regarding the various periods of theatrical art. The lithographs, with one exception, do not illustrate any particular actor or play, but are an attempt to indicate the style of costume and *décor* of the various periods. The exception, which is at p. 117, is based on a surrealist setting for the *Orestes* of Euripides designed by Margaret Souttar and produced at the Barn Theatre, Shere. I wish to acknowledge her kindness in granting me permission to make this use of her design.

J. C.

# CONTENTS

# ILLUSTRATIONS

# THE THEATRE THROUGH THE AGES

# ILLUSTRATIONS

# THE THEATRE THROUGH THE AGES

# CHAPTER ONE

## The Greeks and the Romans

*Plate I*

---

*A Greek Tragedy*

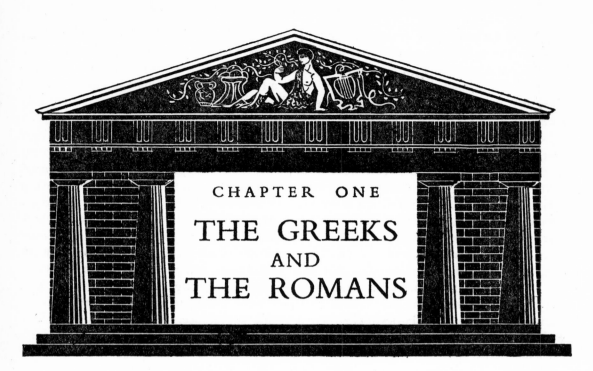

# CHAPTER ONE

# THE GREEKS
## AND
# THE ROMANS

THE THEATRE, AS WE KNOW IT TO-DAY, has its origins, with so much of our Western civilization, in the early days of Greece. Dionysus, or Bacchus, as the Romans called him, was the god of wine and fertility, and every year the Greeks held a number of festivals in his honour. On these occasions the worship of Dionysus took the form of a combination of song and dance, accompanied by music and much flowing of wine. These festivities, at first improvised in a spirit of lively religious fervour, became formalized in the seventh century B.C. by a poet named Arion. Dionysus was supposed to have been enclosed in the thigh of Zeus, the father of all the gods, and then reborn, and so the name 'dithyramb,' meaning twice-born, was given to the poem composed in his honour. The dithyrambs were performed by a chorus of fifty men, who were dressed as satyrs. Their costume was a shaggy goat-skin, embellished with a horse's tail and worn round the middle, and they wore a mask with a snub nose, a beard, and long, animal-like ears. They also wore the phallus, a representation of the male organs, which had a purely symbolical nature in the religion of the Greeks. The chorus did not impersonate the character of the satyr, but looked upon their costumes rather as the outward trappings of their religion.

The idea of impersonation is popularly supposed to have been the innovation of Thespis, a leader of the satyr chorus about 550 B.C. Instead of wearing the satyr's costume, he donned the traditional costume of Hermes, but retained his satyr's mask. The next step was for him to wear the mask of Hermes, and so he became for the first time a definite character, and as such was separated from the chorus, who appointed another leader. Dialogue between the actor (as Thespis had become) and the chorus was then introduced. The actor gradually developed his scope and impersonated other gods, and also the heroes of ancient Greek legend. The subject of all the early plays, then, was, primarily, the life and adventures of Dionysus and, secondly, the ancient epics of Homer. On many of the Greek vases that have survived the painted decoration gives us much information concerning the Greek theatre; Thespis is usually depicted seated in a cart, and for this reason all touring actors have subsequently been known as Thespians.

None of the plays of Thespis has survived; the first great writer for the theatre whose work we know to-day was Æschylus, who lived from 525 to 456 B.C. Æschylus wrote over seventy plays, of which only seven have come down to us. They were all tragedies, comedy being a much later development, and fortunately those that have survived were written at various periods of Æschylus' life, and are very representative of his whole work. From the simple arrangement of chorus, and one actor reciting long lyrical passages of an epic poem, Æschylus developed a more creative and living drama. In *The Persians*, one of his earliest plays, he introduced a second actor, and consequently much more dialogue. As his work developed more characters crept in, and stage effects were inaugurated. Simple properties and settings were introduced; an altar or a tomb, for instance, gave point to the action of one particular part of the play, while trumpets were blown to emphasize other points. Ghostly apparitions and Furies made their dramatic appearance. Æschylus is also credited with the use of paintings, not as a pictorial background to the actors, but as a symbol for a particular scene.

The rapid development of the theatre in the fifth century B.C. was, of course, not due entirely to the innovations of Æschylus. Plays were selected for production in open competition. The city or state authorities, who governed all theatrical activities, would invite poets to submit plays for a coming festival, and to have a play accepted became a great honour. The first great rival of Æschylus was Sophocles, who first appeared as a protagonist in the competitions in 471 B.C. He wrote well over a hundred plays, but, as with Æschylus, only seven survive. His first success was in 468 B.C., when his work was chosen in preference to that of Æschylus. Sophocles actually helped in the development of Æschylus as a playwright, as the older man adopted some of Sophocles' innovations. It was Sophocles who introduced the third actor, and in 458 B.C. Æschylus followed suit in the *Oresteia*. Euripides followed Sophocles as the third great tragic poet. He did not achieve the early success of his predecessors, and had a hard struggle before his plays were accepted; three years after his first victory in the competitions he was defeated again by Sophocles.

The next stage was the growth of comedy, which followed quite naturally after the development of tragedy. Tragedy transported the enrapt audience into the past; it made them sad, and it made them weep. Comedy brought them down to earth; they wiped their eyes, began to smile, and, finally, laughed uproariously. The performances lasted three days, and three tragedies were given each day. The performances would begin at sunrise and continue without a break throughout the day until the early evening, when a short interval for refreshment would be given. After this the performance of a comedy was given, at the conclusion of which the citizens would return to their homes in joyful mood.

Aristophanes was the great writer of comedies, whose extant work was produced from

425 to 388 B.C. His plays were particularly noted for their outspoken topical allusions to unpopular people and causes, for which he suffered imprisonment several times in the course of his career.

Although these four writers are the great figures of Greek drama, their achievements were probably due in no small measure to the spirit of competition which was the basis of all Dionysiac festivals. The State selected the poets who were to take part in the competitions. For the tragedies usually three poets were selected; for the comedies, in later times, the number was five. There were ten judges, who were selected from the citizens, partly by election and partly by appointment. The judges sat in seats of honour in the front rows of the theatre, and after the conclusion of the performances made their choice, placing their votes in an urn. From the urn only five selections were taken, and the majority of these decided the final result of the competition. To win victory in the competition was considered a great honour, and the poet's name was inscribed in the public archives and carved on a tablet in the theatre. The prize was originally a goat for the winning tragic poet, and for the writer of the winning comedies a basket of figs and a jar of wine. Later, however, money prizes were given. The lively spirit of the competitions kept the poets very active, and stimulated the production of their best efforts throughout their lives. Æschylus died at the age of sixty-nine, and was producing plays right up to a few years before his death. Both Sophocles and Euripides also produced plays late in life.

The drama in Greece, then, arose from the religious festivals, of which there were four during the year. Only two of these, however, were associated with dramatic performances: the Lenæa and the City Dionysia, as they were called. Comedies were given at both festivals, but tragedies were presented only at the chief festival, the City Dionysia, which was held in the early spring. The festival would begin with a procession through the city of the priests, the officials, the poets, the actors, the choregi (the wealthy citizens who were called upon to finance the productions as a State tax), the members of the various choruses, and the musicians, followed by the populace of the city and the many strangers who had come to join in the celebrations. Attired in brilliantly coloured garments, richly ornamented with gold, the procession would march to the temple of Dionysus, carry out the statue of the god, and set him up in state in the theatre. Announcements would then be made of the plays to be performed on the following day.

The performances were usually preceded by the choral competitions, in which choruses of men and boys sang as representatives of the various communities in the State. After this the poet came forward and announced his plays which were to be performed that day. The plays were then given. The audiences of those days could sit on stone benches through a whole day, from sunrise to sunset, with only one interval, in rapt attention to the spectacle before them and the alternating voices of actor and chorus. That this was possible was, in the first place, a triumph of art, and in the second a measure of the extraordinary enthusiasm of all members of the State. Perhaps religious fervour had something to do with it, but the plays of the great poets of the fifth century B.C. would seem to have little in common with the wine-induced ecstasy of the early Dionysiac festivals. The performances would continue on the following days, and the judges would then make their choice of the winning and second-best poets. The winning poet would be brought on to the stage and crowned with a chaplet of ivy, a solemn sacrifice would be made, and the proceedings would be wound up with a grand banquet given by him to his actors, chorus, and friends.

The theatre belonged to the State, and a public official called the archon had the responsibility of bringing the various people together in order to produce a play. The poets were selected previously by the State; then the actors, who were also paid by the State, were attached to the poets by lot. No poet was allowed to choose his own actors—a condition which was a constant source of worry to the poets. The State then nominated to each poet a choregus, who was called upon to finance the production, paying the chorus, the supers, and the musicians, providing the costumes and properties, and meeting all expenses involved in the performances. Here, again, the poet had his worries, for a niggardly choregus would not spend more than he thought necessary, and on the actual mounting of the play might depend the judges' verdict. The system became more practical when the choregus was also honoured along with the winning poet, for, generally speaking, the choregi coveted the honour, and consequently went to considerable expense to have the best chorus and costumes available. Nicias and Antisthenes were two choregi who spent money lavishly, and with their poets won many victories in the competitions.

Although there were only three actors in each play, a considerable number of what we should call 'supers' were used as soldiers, attendants, and other characters who appeared on the stage, but were not required to speak. The chorus for the tragedies was composed of fifteen men, who were all highly trained in declamation, music, and dancing. In the comedies the chorus was rather larger, and the number was generally twenty-four. The choregi had to pay the chorus a wage, provide their keep, and attend to their training. In the days of the great poets they themselves would train the chorus, but after Euripides they no longer took an active part in production, and a special chorus-trainer was appointed, thus causing a further drain on the resources of the choregi. During the time of the Peloponnesian Wars, when money was rather scarce, the authorities allowed the expenses of each play to be shared by two or more choregi; and eventually, at the end of the fourth century B.C., the State took over complete responsibility, and bore the entire cost.

Originally the performances were given to the entire population free of charge. The consequence was that people would arrive at the theatre the day before the performances to take the best seats. There were also many complaints about foreigners taking all the seats, so the State decided to charge a small fee, and issued tickets for the seats. All citizens, however poor, were entitled to see the plays, and in cases of dire need the State officials provided the cost of admission. As the performances were part of a sacred festival, even prisoners were released from gaol in order that they might attend. During the several days of the festival all citizens were expected to be on their best behaviour, any offences committed during the period being punished severely and the offenders publicly castigated at the close of the festival.

As there were few books and only a small proportion of the people could read, the plays, with their largely historic content, had a useful educational value; the poet, therefore, exercised considerable influence on the people in the rôle of teacher. During the sixth and fifth centuries successful plays were given only one performance, with the exception of the plays of Æschylus, which were continually revived after his death. The poets who were unsuccessful in the competitions were allowed to revise or rewrite their plays and submit them again at subsequent festivals. Euripides gained several victories with plays which had been rewritten after unsuccessful performances. The fourth century produced no great tragic writers, and so the revival of the old plays became a regular custom. This being the period when the art of acting reached its highest level, the old plays, being well known (so that interpretation became more important), sometimes suffered under the drastic adaptation carried out by certain actors.

The early theatres were temporary affairs, consisting of a wooden platform used as a

A GREEK AMPHITHEATRE

stage, with a tent or booth at the rear for the use of the actors, while the audience sat on rough wooden benches. About the time of Thespis the theatre had become more permanent; the platform and booth had developed into permanent stage buildings and the wooden benches into a stone amphitheatre. The theatre at Athens was the original of all the ancient theatres. Building began about 500 B.C., and work continued for nearly two hundred years. A natural position on a hillside was chosen for the site, the rows of stone seats following the contours of the ground rising up the hill, and roughly forming the shape of a horseshoe. In the centre was the circular orchestra, or dancing place, in which the chorus performed, and behind was the stage, a platform which, though wide, was only a few feet in depth. Behind the stage was the façade of the stage buildings, embellished with columns and other architectural features. In the centre was a large door, flanked on either side by one or two smaller doors, all of which were used by the actors when making their entrances and exits. The theatre at Athens faced south, and a convention arose out of the natural position of the stage. To the right of the stage was the distant sea, and to the left the country inland. When a character in a play was supposed to come from a distant land across the sea the actor would make his entrance from the right-hand door, and, conversely, it would seem quite natural for a character coming from the near-by countryside to make his entrance from the left-hand door. The chorus also used the side-doors to come down into the orchestra. In later times, when the chorus occasionally took part in the action on the stage, as in the plays of Aristophanes, a temporary wooden staircase was erected in the centre of the stage. As the stage was nearly twelve feet higher than the orchestra, the use of this staircase must have been a rather awkward procedure. Generally the chorus remained below in the circular orchestra, and the dialogue between chorus and actors took place with the actors speaking from the stage and the chorus from below. While the actors were speaking the chorus stood with their backs to the audience, facing the stage, and when their turn to speak arrived they turned and faced the audience—a simple, formal arrangement, which gave emphasis to various parts of the play.

The stage buildings at the back of the stage were as high as the last row of seats in the amphitheatre; this was an arrangement which suited the excellent acoustic properties of the theatre. The audience were entirely at the mercy of the weather, there being no protection from sun or rain, but as the performances were held in the early spring the sun would be rather welcome and the rain the only trouble.

Mention has been made of Æschylus using painted scenery as a background to the presentation of his plays. There is little knowledge of its specific use, but information is available of certain scenic devices, which were used not in the modern pictorial fashion, but rather in a symbolic sense. On each side of the stage was erected a three-sided screen, on which were painted three different pictures. The screens were made to revolve so that any of the three pictures could face the audience. It is not known whether a backcloth was used in the early days, but its use certainly developed in Roman times. The simple arrangement of easily changed pictures would give the audience sufficient understanding of a change of scene. The revolving of one screen alone meant that the scene represented was in the immediate neighbourhood of the preceding scene, while the movement of both screens represented a complete change of locality. Most of the plays of Sophocles and Euripides have their scenes laid before a temple or palace, and the stage buildings, with their columns, thus formed a very suitable background. If a backcloth was used it would have been in two sections, the lower part painted to represent buildings or natural surroundings, and the upper part to represent the sky. This was because in many of the plays an actor personifying a god often made his appearance at the top of the buildings. The complicated tangle of plots and counter-plots in Euripides is usually straightened out towards the end of the play by a god making his appearance out of the sky. Sometimes a crane was used to convey him to the ground or stage-level, and also to carry characters such as Trygæus, in Aristophanes' *The Peace*, who, in order to meet the gods, flew up to Olympus on the back of a giant beetle. The use of this contrivance originated the phrase *deus ex machina*, which has come to mean a device introduced in order to bring the action of a play to a convenient, if artificial, conclusion.

Another device frequently used by the Greeks was a trolley, which was pushed out on to the stage through the large central door, and on which a tableau of characters would be arranged. Scenes of violence were taboo in the Greek theatre, and all murders were committed off-stage. As all scenes were exteriors, any important action in a play taking place indoors was also conveyed to the audience by the expedient of pushing out the trolley with the characters in a set pose. There was no attempt at realism, but a simple use of stage convention, which, once established, could be employed with great dramatic effect.

Trap-doors were also used in bringing ghosts, Furies, and other subterranean beings on to the stage. Certain properties were continually used as part of the setting, altars and tombs and statues of gods being constantly referred to in the Greek plays. In much later times horses and chariots were brought on to the stage. The theatre at Epidaurus, which is considered the most beautiful of the ancient theatres, had a stage which, although only eight feet deep, was seventy-eight feet wide, thus making it quite easy to gallop a horse or bring a chariot across. The rush of movement so caused would create a dramatic contrast to the rather static performance of the actors; nevertheless this practice was never widely used, and remained something of a novelty. There were only three actors in a Greek play, but there were, of course, many characters, both male and female, and so each actor was called upon to play a number of parts. The great advantage of this system was that even the minor parts were excellently played. There were never more than three characters involved in dialogue together; if a fourth character did appear on the stage it had no lines to speak, and so the part could be played by a super or a minor actor. In their representation of characters the actors wore masks and costumes, which made it simple to change from one character to another.

The continual change of character did, of course, stress the importance of the actor's voice. It had primarily to be powerful, as the theatre held nearly thirty thousand spectators, and it had to be flexible, to change with the character—from youth to old age, and from man to woman. Some actors could imitate all kinds of weird noises: the rush of the wind, the roar of the seas, and a whole repertoire of animal cries. Actors of bad taste would indulge any abilities they had in this direction, as it was always a sure method of attracting applause. Writers of discernment deplored this rather cheap method of winning over an audience, and

Aristotle, when writing of the tragic actor Theodorus, commends the thoroughly natural quality of his voice, saying that, unlike other actors, he seemed to speak with his own voice. Tragic plays were delivered in a loud and sonorous style, and all movements were dignified and restrained, while in comedy a more conversational style was used and the movements were much more active.

Acting reached its height of achievement during the fourth century, particularly as the old tragedies could be revived, and their interpretation assumed new importance. After Euripides, as we have already pointed out, there was a decline in the use of the chorus by

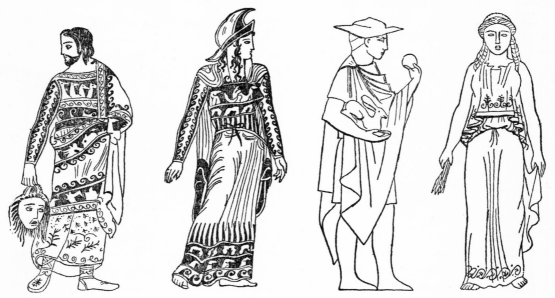

GREEK STAGE COSTUMES FOR TRAGEDY      GREEK EVERYDAY COSTUME

the tragic writers, and more dialogue was given to the actors. The actors' professional status was regarded as an honourable one, almost comparable with that of the priests; and as they wished to maintain their privileges, they formed a guild in about the middle of the fourth century. The Artists of Dionysus, as they were called, brought in as members of the guild poets, actors, chorus and trainers, and musicians. Among the privileges they were granted was permission to travel through foreign, and even hostile, states to give performances. Two famous actors travelled from Athens to Macedonia during the height of the war against Philip of Macedon to give performances, and they actually assisted in negotiating the peace. Another privilege they obtained from the State, though not without some trouble, was exemption from the compulsory period of military service.

The costumes of Greek tragedy were neither strictly historical nor contemporary, and although the action of the tragedies took place in Homeric times, there was no attempt at historical accuracy. At the same time the Greeks considered that the common, everyday dress was not sufficiently dignified to be worn by their gods and heroes; so a special costume

TRAGIC HERO

TRAGIC HEROINE

MESSENGER

OLD MAN, NEW COMEDY

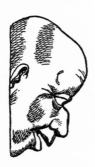

PARASITE

COURTESAN

SOME MASKS OF THE GREEK STAGE

was evolved. A long-sleeved robe decorated with bright colours was the basis of the costume. With this would be worn either the himation, a long mantle usually worn over the right shoulder and covering most of the body, or the chlamys, a short cloak which was flung across the left shoulder. Buskins with high soles of six inches or more gave the actor greater height and dignity, while the mask gave the clue to the character. Thespis is supposed to have invented the tragic mask, although Æschylus and others developed its use. The characters in Greek tragedies are general types rather than individuals, and so a certain number of set masks was evolved. They indicated by simple outline and shape the general attributes of the particular character. Facial expression, which is so important in the actor's craft to-day, was quite out of the question in the enormous Greek theatres. Once the masks were evolved they changed only in detail throughout the centuries. The masks varied in size according to the importance of the character, and the coiffure was built up from the forehead accordingly. That is to say, a king's mask would have the hair built up considerably, the actor thus gaining more inches in height, while the mask of a minor character would have no such 'built-up' effect. The masks were originally made of stiffened linen, but later it was found that cork or wood had better acoustic properties. Some masks had a small megaphone arrangement concealed inside the open mouth, which amplified the voice of the actor to some degree. The masks entirely covered the head, and were painted to emphasize the expression and to delineate the character further; even the eye was painted in, with only a small hole through which the actor could see.

With the extra height gained by the use of buskin and the size of the mask, the body of the actor tended to look puny, so that it was necessary to pad out the costumes to equalize matters. The trailing gowns worn by women characters were longer than the men's, and were usually of a particular colour; a queen's costume, for instance, was purple. In the days when theatre programmes were unheard of it was important that the audience should recognize a character at once, and therefore if certain characters were always dressed in a costume of a particular colour recognition was easy. Colour was also used to signify the condition of a character; if in misfortune or exile, a mantle of black or grey would be worn over the tunic. In Greece hats were worn only when on a journey, and so the audience could readily appreciate the change of scene implied when a hatted character appeared. All the male characters in tragedies wore the same kind of tunic, girdled high up under the breast and falling in long, graceful folds. The tunics differed only in decoration, which was designed in patterns of varied colours. These patterns were based on floral designs or simply drawn animal or bird shapes. To differentiate among gods and heroes certain easily recognizable properties were carried; thus Apollo had his bow, Hermes his magic wand, Hercules his club and lion-skin, and Perseus his cap of darkness. Warriors usually appeared in full armour, with a short cloak of scarlet wrapped round the arm. Old men carried a bent staff, and messengers of good tidings wore crowns of olive or laurel. Kings wore a crown and carried a sceptre, and they also wore an extra short tunic over the usual long one.

The costume of comedy was rather different, the tunics being much shorter and with much padding fore and aft. The tradition of the old boisterous Dionysiac festivals was continued by the wearing of the phallus. In the plays of Aristophanes the chorus in some cases did

22

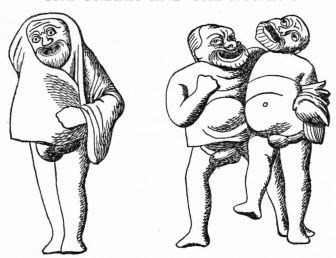

STATUETTES OF GREEK COMIC ACTORS

not represent human beings, and so special costumes were used. At times other writers used this device, and the chorus were represented as birds, fishes, insects, frogs, goats, and even clouds. In *The Birds* of Aristophanes the chorus wore a delightfully conventionalized bird costume, complete with wings and crests. The buskin was never worn in comedy, a soft-soled shoe known as the soccus being introduced, which has always since been associated with comic acting.

CHORUS COSTUMES FOR "THE BIRDS"

23

Towards the end of the fourth century B.C., when Athens had lost its political importance, but still held the lead in art, science, and philosophy, the last important development took place in Greek drama. The subject of comedy shifted from the satirical political themes of Aristophanes to scenes of domestic everyday life. Athens, no longer a democracy, was now under the domination of Macedonia, and the freedom of speech enjoyed by Aristophanes was no longer possible. Political reasons, then, conditioned the creation of the New Comedy, as it has been called. The greatest writer of New Comedy was Menander (343–292), who wrote over a hundred plays, of which only fragments have survived. Menander's comedies had certain typical figures or stock types, and the costumes approximated more closely to everyday life, although the convention of using certain colours to give the clue to the character still held good. A character which appeared in most of the plays was the roguish slave, who had a very distinctive mask and red hair, and wore a short white tunic. Old men also wore white, and were always clean-shaven, with closely cropped hair. Beards were worn only to denote mature manhood or middle age. Young men wore purple, parasites black or grey, and old women yellow or light blue. Courtesans were easily recognized by having their hair bound up with golden ornaments and brightly coloured bands. The actors of New Comedy, by discarding the phallus and wearing costumes similar to the everyday garb of the Greeks, developed a more realistic style of acting. They appeared in amusing situations and developed a more individualistic style of acting. It was inevitable that the general theme of the plays was that of human failings and vanities. The dissolute rake of wealthy parents with his amorous adventures—largely engineered by his slave—the courtesan, the stern parent, and the seduced daughter were all typical figures. The tragedies of the past were still being revived at this period, but the old comedies were dead and buried and New Comedy reigned in their stead.

The chorus reached its peak of importance under Euripides, when it consisted of fifteen men. These moved in a military formation of three files, each of five men, and were usually characterized as old men, women, or maidens, being generally supposed to represent the 'public.' They wore masks, and their dress was usually contemporary, except, as mentioned previously, when they were not representing human beings. In the *Eumenides* of Æschylus they were dressed in black costumes and wore masks with distorted features, while artificial snakes were entangled in their hair. Normally the chorus was grouped in a rectangular formation in the circular orchestra, and had various forms of delivery. They either sang, spoke, or delivered their lines in the form of recitative, accompanied by a flute. The chorus was also required to perform various dances, those of the tragic plays being slow and dignified, while in the comedies the movements were more lively, and often lascivious and coarse. All singing in those days was in unison, harmony having yet to be discovered, and the music was written to suit the words. Remembering that it was chiefly the lyrical parts of the play that were allocated to the chorus, it will be seen that all dancing and music was subordinated to the poetry. The members of the chorus had to be highly skilled men, and the leader had a position almost as important as the actor's. It was necessary for the chorus to be well trained, not only as individuals, but also as a group, and their attainments must have been a considerable contribution to the stature of Greek drama.

Audiences at the theatre at Athens numbered nearly thirty thousand, and included strangers and foreigners who were attracted to the festivals. Ambassadors and representatives of allied states came to pay the annual tributes, sums of money which were displayed on the stage. The front rows of the theatre were reserved for these important people, and also for the various priests, the State officials, and the judges. The priest of Dionysus had a throne of honour in the centre of the front row, and there were other thrones set up for the rest of the officials. Successful generals also sat among the *élite*. The remainder of the seats in the theatre were backless stone benches, built very close together. Rich men brought rugs and cushions, and no doubt proved very unpopular with the more democratic citizens. The Athenians were a very lively audience, and it was necessary to have a team of staff-bearers to keep order. They patrolled up and down the narrow gangways which divided the audience into twelve blocks. Although in Greece at that time it was customary to relegate women to seclusion, they were allowed to see the performances. They all sat together in one place, probably at the back of the theatre. Boys were also admitted, and they

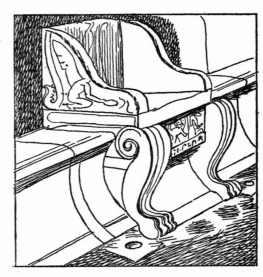

THRONE OF HONOUR FOR THE
PRIEST OF DIONYSUS

too had their special place in the auditorium. Slaves were sometimes taken when they were lucky enough to have a benevolent master. Among the audience of the Greek theatre were types which will always be found throughout the ages. There was the man of taste and discernment, who hissed when every one else was applauding and clapped when every one else was silent. There was the boy who continually whistled the popular tunes, and the young man of the city who took pleasure in hissing a play off the stage.

Aristotle divides the audiences into two parts: the refined and cultured citizens and the rough and ignorant artisans; and it is interesting in the study of Greek drama to see how the poets have met the two almost contradictory demands. Superb poetry goes with simple and sometimes very amusing stage devices, and the sublime is very happily wedded to the ridiculous.

The young and aggressive Roman republic borrowed its drama, like most of its art, from the Greeks. About the middle of the third century B.C. Livius Andronicus presented a comedy and a tragedy in Rome, which had been adapted from the Greek and translated into Latin, and the success of these performances ensured that future plays should be modelled on those of the Greeks. He had been taken captive as a child and brought to Rome as a slave. His command of both Latin and Greek enabled him to become a tutor and eventually a freedman. He translated the tragedies of Sophocles and Euripides as well as some Greek comedies.

Nævius, a contemporary of Livius Andronicus, also translated many of the old plays. Consequently the Roman playwrights had the advantage of ready-made material, an advantage which they certainly took. Plautus and Terence borrowed wholesale from the New Comedy of Menander, and most of our knowledge of his work is based on the study of their plays. Seneca wrote tragedy which was to prove the model for all subsequent periods in the theatre, notably the Elizabethan playwrights in England and the French theatre of the seventeenth century.

Roman dramatic performances were not altogether religious festivals, but often merely public holidays or special performances in honour of victorious generals. The number of official holidays at which dramatic performances took place steadily increased through the years until in A.D. 354 there were over a hundred days set aside for that purpose. On some occasions after the victorious return of an expedition the spoils of war were carried by hundreds of mules across the stage—a spectacle which may have delighted the multitude, but was to the intelligent writer of the time, as Cicero, for instance, a boring substitute for drama. The theatres changed considerably under Roman influence, and eventually all the ancient theatres were adapted to the new conditions. The use of the chorus further declined, and the orchestra subsequently became smaller. The new theatres built by the Romans differed fundamentally from those of the Greeks in that they were usually built on level ground instead of on a hillside. The reason for this, it has been suggested, is the love of architectural embellishment, which the Romans were able to lavish on the outside walls of these theatres.

The stage was provided with a sloping roof, which probably acted as a sounding-board

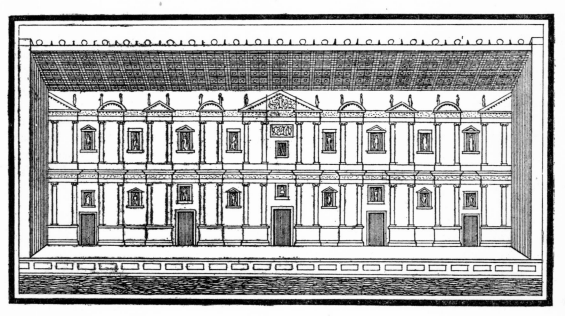

A ROMAN STAGE

26

and improved the acoustics. The stage was also enlarged, and the façade of the stage buildings elaborated with many statues and architectural features. Eventually the Romans abolished the choral part of the performances, and all spectacle took place on the stage. A curtain was introduced to mark the beginning and end of the play. Instead of being raised to open the play, the curtain was lowered, a slit-trench being excavated in the floor of the stage to house it during the performance. Details of the arrangements for working the curtain are not available, but probably pulleys were attached to the roof of the stage and the ropes went through to the rear of the stage buildings. As dramatic performances in Rome went on throughout the year, huge canvas awnings were erected to give shelter to the audience.

Under the Romans tragedy and comedy declined in favour of farces, burlesques, and pantomime, which were nearer the vaudeville shows of our own time. In place of the tragedies solo performances were given by tragedians or famous personalities. Nero himself delighted in giving tragic recitations, and he appeared on the stage as Apollo, Hercules, Orestes, and the blinded Œdipus, accompanying himself on the cither.

The Greeks had laid great stress on the unity of production: actors, chorus, and musicians worked together in perfect harmony as a team. The Romans made more of individual performances of the leading actors. Until the first century B.C. the Roman actors played without masks and specialized in one particular kind of rôle. This meant that the original three actors of the Greek tragedies, who played in turn many parts, switching from one character to another by changing masks, gave way to a troupe of specialists in the various rôles of women, old men, youths, and parasites. Without masks the Roman actors were able to develop facial expression, which led to further specialization. The Romans were born improvisers, and with their lively and expressive gestures took naturally to the stage. Acting reached its heights of perfection in Rome when the writing of plays was in its decline, during the first century B.C.

The greatest actor the Romans produced was Roscius, who specialized in comedy. When drama had begun to decline in favour of spectacle he reintroduced many of the ancient Greek customs, including the use of masks, and succeeded in re-establishing the individuality of the actor. His name has subsequently always been associated with the height of perfection in acting. In spite of Roscius, however, the acting profession lost its status under the Romans. Actors even lost their elementary rights as citizens, and were considered little better than slaves. This was partly due to managers forming permanent troupes consisting of slaves whom they could treat as they wished. Floggings and beatings were the reward of such actors should they not be well received and thus bring subsequent discredit on the manager. In the Roman theatre most of the acting profession were probably of foreign extraction and mostly slaves, while a few of the leading actors may have been freedmen who very occasionally received civic honours. Women appeared in dramatic performances, chiefly as dancers and instrumentalists, a thing unheard of in the days of the Greeks.

The Romans differed greatly from the Greeks in their love of bloodshed and scenes of violence. Actors were made to resort to kicks and blows in their performances. Ear-boxing, acrobatic feats, and juggling with knives became common accomplishments. Sometimes scores of warriors, mounted and in full armour, presented mimic battles. These gave way to the actuality of gladiatorial fights and animal baitings. Life was cheap in the days of the Empire, and slaves, captives, and robbers were thrown to their deaths to wild beasts made ferocious by judicious starving. Sometimes the unfortunate victims were made subject to dramatic performances which culminated in their execution. At the time of Trajan a musician dressed as Orpheus was torn to pieces by wild animals; while on the day Caligula was murdered, during the performance of a mime, a robber was brought on to the stage and actually nailed to a cross, the audience apparently enjoying his slow and painful death. In later times the robbers and slaves were replaced as victims by the early Christian martyrs. The worst effect of Roman life on the theatre was not the decay of acting and drama, but such degenerate spectacles.

# CHAPTER TWO

# The Middle Ages and the Renaissance

*Plate II*

---

*Scene from a Miracle Play in
the Middle Ages*

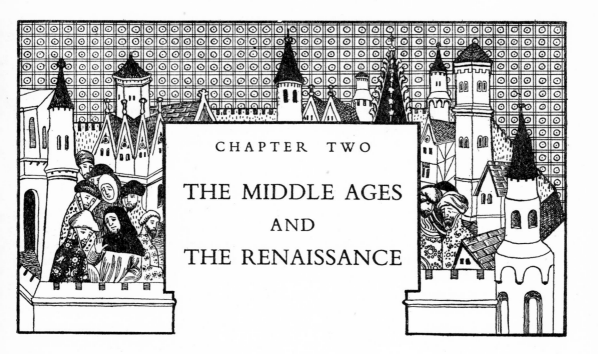

# CHAPTER TWO

# THE MIDDLE AGES
# AND
# THE RENAISSANCE

WITH THE DECLINE OF THE ROMAN EMPIRE came the breaking-up of all the dramatic traditions inherited from the Greeks. The theatres, however, continued to flourish. They had become a very popular feature in the life of the Romans, and their numbers grew from forty-eight under Augustus to over a hundred under Constantine. They were very large, and each was capable of holding tens of thousands of the polyglot peoples living within the Roman Empire. Apart from being the source of entertainment, they were the only meeting-place for slaves and people without rights, who were debarred from forum and senate. In addition to being the rallying-point for possible disturbers of the peace, the theatre was also a convenient instrument for winning over the populace. For these reasons the authorities tightened their control over the theatres and passed many laws imposing restrictions on the actors. They were treated little better than slaves, and both Julius Cæsar and Augustus enforced laws which in effect deprived them of their civic rights.

The large popular audiences did not care much for literary drama, and the numerous tongues spoken in the Empire dismissed the possibility of any subtlety in the performances. There arose from these conditions a new form of entertainment, the mime. It was found expedient to have intervals in the long tragic dramas, during which certain actors would come forward and perform a short interlude, in which singing, dancing, and acrobatics were mingled with dialogue. The subject of these so-called farces was to be found in the low life of the times. There developed certain stock types—*i.e.*, a fat, talkative fool, a malicious character, a stupid rustic fool, a foolish old man, and, as women also played in the mimes, equivalent female rôles. The dialogue was usually improvised, and naturally had a close relationship to contemporary life. The mimes became so popular that they expanded, and became the principal part of the programme. They achieved success for the same reason that variety is popular to-day, because of the intensely human qualities contained in their vulgarity. The actors in the mimes wore short tunics with a yellow or parti-coloured cloak, and they generally discarded the traditional mask. There is a tradition that the actresses played in the nude, and although this probably was not general, it certainly is conceivable that this might have happened when we consider the way the Romans lived during the late years of the Empire. Furthermore, it is hardly necessary to point out the fact of the nudes on our own variety stage.

The tragic actors were themselves influenced by the mimes, and had to adopt the new technique. The long lyrical passages in the tragic plays were now sung by one player, accompanied by musicians, while the actor spoke the dialogue only. Later the dialogue was completely dropped by the actors, who now concentrated on miming the action, while a large choir sang or chanted the story. The histriones, as the tragic actors were now called, were in continual rivalry with the mimes until the last years of the Empire, when in order to survive the growing difficulties they merged together.

By far the greatest opposition to theatres and actors in general came from the early Christian leaders, and as Christianity spread it began to have some influence in the civil legislation of the Empire. In the fourth century A.D. the so-called *Canons of Hippolytus*, presumed to be the work of the leader of the Christian Church at that time, prohibited the theatre to the clergy. Also, the players had to quit their profession if they wanted to become Christians, or even if they wanted to marry a Christian. The Church forbade theatrical performances on Sundays and on religious festival days. St John Chrysostom in the East and St Jerome in the West continued to issue edicts on the evils of the theatres. In spite of this growing opposition the theatres continued, and during the last years of the Empire there was actually a lessening of official restrictions. This may have been partly due to the Emperor Justinian, whose wife Theodora had been an actress in the past, before becoming his mistress and, subsequently, his wife and Empress.

By A.D. 400 the theatres were doomed, not because of early Christian opposition, but from an entirely new danger. Within a few years Rome was sacked by the invading Goths, and in order to find a scapegoat for their defeat, the authorities blamed the degeneration of the Roman defenders on the loose morals of the theatre. But in A.D. 467 Rome was again sacked, and yet a theatre was still there. Theodoric, the Ostrogoth who invaded Italy in 488, found it expedient to continue the theatres, and they had further years of grace until 568, when the Lombards, the hard, tough Germans from the north, descended on Italy; after this, although the Lombards did not conquer the city itself, there is no more mention of theatres in Rome.

Theatrical performances, however, did not come to an end. Although the actors had to leave the theatres, they formed small companies which took to the roads and wandered through the country, from hamlet to village and city, giving private performances at weddings, baptisms, and other festivities. Even though the theatres were closed, the Church showed itself still alive to the evils of the stage, and the officiating clergy would be ordered to leave before the actors began their performance.

For centuries the actors wandered the roads, rubbing shoulders with acrobats, rope-dancers, and beast-tamers. The best of them became minstrels and gleemen, the well-paid servants of nobles and kings. The rest merged with the lower class of entertainers and were little better than wandering vagabonds. The earliest English poem is about a famous minstrel named Widsith, an epic singer who wandered across Europe to Egypt, Persia, and even as far as India. The minstrels and gleemen were well established in England by the time Christianity came, in the sixth century. Their performances were in the nature of songs sung in praise of heroes and great deeds, and during the Middle Ages, when Europe was continually at war, they had no difficulty in finding the necessary material. Wandering minstrels were usually made very welcome wherever they stayed. They had practically a free right of entry into all the great houses and castles of the nobles of the land. For in addition to entertainment, they also brought news of foreign parts, which, no doubt, they carefully coloured to suit their particular audience. Sometimes they would settle down permanently in the service of a king or noble.

The Church looked with disfavour on the activities of the minstrels, and the bishops were continually issuing orders prohibiting the clergy from welcoming or watching the performers. A priest of Ripon minster was charged, in 1312, with breaking the canons in this respect. In spite of the edicts of the bishops, however, the clergy looked forward to occasional visits from wandering minstrels, even certain bishops receiving them favourably, and they were usually assured of a warm welcome in the monasteries. The clergy, of course, were only human, and the minstrels certainly satisfied the very human need of news and entertainment. By the eleventh century the minstrels were popular among all classes, and they gave their performances in tavern, castle, guild-hall, and market-place. At festivities such as weddings they appeared in great strength; there were four hundred and twenty-six of them at the marriage of Margaret of England and John of Brabant in 1290. Some of the more famous minstrels made large sums of money. Rahere, who was chief minstrel to Henry I, made a fortune, and, deciding to quit the profession, founded the great priory of St Bartholomew, of which he became the first prior.

In France, at Beauvais, Lyons, and Cambrai, were some famous minstrel schools, where minstrels from all over Europe would gather during Lent, when no performances were given. There they would learn new songs and fresh news and material.

The first requirement for a successful minstrel was a pleasing voice and personality, and the second a suitable accompaniment. The usual accompanying instruments were the harp and a fiddle-like instrument known as the vielle. Trumpets were also used, not so much as an accompaniment as for sounding fanfares to punctuate the dramatic moments of the performance. Other instruments of the time were a kind of hand organ, cithers of various shapes and sizes, bagpipes, drums, and cymbals. When several minstrels performed together they sang alternately in the form of dialogue, based on question and answer. There are many illustrations in old illuminated manuscripts of minstrels and musicians and other entertainers of the Middle Ages wearing the usual costume of the period, but in much bolder

MINSTRELS IN THE MIDDLE AGES

colours and decoration. We can well imagine them presenting a pleasing and colourful entertainment to the simple, illiterate people of the time. Certain stage properties, such as the old favourite, the ass's head, were common, and animal mimicry reached a fine art.

At the beginning of the fifteenth century there were small groups of minstrels in the service of the municipal corporations of the larger towns, such as London, Bristol, York, Canterbury, Shrewsbury, Chester, and Norwich. They wore the town livery and played at local festivities and celebrations. The 'waits,' as they were called, had other duties to perform, including the very odious one of piping the watch at certain fixed hours of the night.

The fifteenth century saw the invention of printing, and when books became available in large numbers and the upper classes learnt to read the minstrels saw their popularity waning. They flourished between the eleventh and thirteenth centuries, and had quite disappeared by the sixteenth century. The lower class of entertainer still continued in the market-place, together with the jugglers and acrobats, while some of the best were no doubt absorbed into the companies of stage players that were established in the early sixteenth century.

In spite of the importance and popularity of the minstrels during the Middle Ages the development of the theatre owes more in this period to the activities of the people themselves. The Middle Ages was, indeed, the great period of amateur theatricals. Apart from the folk drama arising out of very ancient celebrations connected with farming and the land, such as the May Day festivals, the Mummers, and the Sword Dance, the chief contribution to the history of the theatre came through the medium of the Church. This drama began in a very simple way, developed and established its own conventions, and brought to the common people that pageantry and entertainment so necessary to relieve the monotony of the daily round and common task.

From 970 onward there are records to show the introduction of drama into church services. It probably came about through the desire of the clergy to make the incidents in the life of Christ appear more real to the congregations. A beginning was made with the Easter morning service, when a short, simple scene was played before the altar. A seat representing the sepulchre would be placed where all could see, with two priests dressed as angels on either side. Three women would enter and wander up to the angels, one of whom then asked, "Whom do you seek in the sepulchre, O Christian women?" They would

MINSTRELS IN THE MIDDLE AGES

reply, "Jesus of Nazareth, who was crucified, O heavenly ones." The angel would say, pointing, "He is not here; He has risen even as He foretold. Go announce that He has arisen from the sepulchre." After this all would join with choir and congregation in *Te Deum Laudamus*, and the church bells would chime out in an effective climax. When treated formally this little scene must have had a tremendous effect on the congregation. The dialogue was chanted in Latin and the angels' wings looked very unconvincing, but such was the pattern of the scene and the earnestness of the players that the performance was really effective. The success of this small beginning was followed by other short scenes, such as the meeting of Mary Magdalene and Christ in the garden, Peter and John running to the sepulchre, and the incredulity of Thomas. Later, at Christmas other scenes were introduced, showing the shepherds, the star, and the three kings at the manger. From being chanted in Latin the dialogue came to be spoken in English, and gradually the religious play evolved, quite separately from the service. The whole interior of the church was used, and short scenes were played in various parts of the building. The setting in each case was symbolized to represent a particular place or scene, and for certain scenes a permanent structure was built in the church. Thus, instead of being represented by a seat, the sepulchre became a wooden or iron construction, complete with hinged lid.

The actors were the people of the church, the priests, nuns, and choir-boys, and their costumes consisted of the usual ecclesiastical dress, the surplices, copes, and chasubles of the times. The beautiful interiors of the early churches provided plenty of opportunity for dramatic effect, and the lighted candles carried by the actors heightened the emphasis on the individual scenes. An example of a twelfth-century Resurrection play shows the various scenes arranged as in the diagram, with the crucifix naturally represented at the altar. The play would begin with the actors performing one scene, possibly near the entrance of the church, and then, having played it, moving on to the next scene, and so on right round the church. The content of these religious plays varied considerably, and incidents from the Old Testament were introduced. The increasing number of scenes, together with the larger congregations the plays attracted, made it necessary to produce the plays outside, on the church steps.

From the thirteenth to the fourteenth centuries the main development was the taking over of the drama from the Church by the people themselves. This was due to the Church authorities resenting the enormous popularity and appeal the performances themselves, as distinct from the Church services, had for the common people. The Church understood the latent power of the drama well enough, and it saw that the people who watched the plays showed no signs of spiritual uplift, but simply came to be entertained. So the Church stopped producing the plays and prohibited the clergy from taking part in them. However, the plays were an accepted part of the Easter celebrations, and the people demanded their entertainment, so the guilds took over the responsibility of production. The various craft guilds, who had also other responsibilities, such as the repair of bridges and roads and the building of chapels and charitable institutions, took their turn in producing the plays and providing the actors, the costumes, and the various scenes and effects. From the steps of the church the spectacle moved to market-place and guild hall.

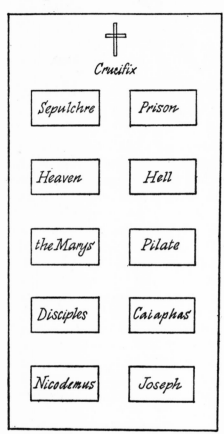

THE LAY-OUT OF THE SCENES IN A TWELFTH-CENTURY RESUR-RECTION PLAY

The guilds took their responsibility for production very seriously, and they spent considerable sums on scenery, costumes, and effects, and even paid the actors for their part in the performance. Thus a man at Coventry was paid 3s. 4d. for playing God, another, 4d. for cock-crowing, while at Hull a certain Jenkin Smith received 1s. 1d. for taking the part of Noah.

The plays grew in length as more scenes from the Old Testament were added, and the performances now lasted several days. The dialogue became more in keeping with daily life, and therefore more easily managed by the simple amateur actors. The plays followed the same tradition of the earlier church performances by having separately erected settings for each scene. The various settings were built of wood and canvas on elevated stages for all to see. If one can imagine a modern fair-ground arranged in a rectangle, with all the side-shows distributed round the sides, and perhaps one or two in the central open space, this will give some idea of the staging of the miracle plays as played on the Continent.

A painting by the artist Jehan Fouquet shows an incident during one of the French miracle plays, and behind the central group of actors can be seen the several stages for the various scenes in the play. One of the most prominent figures in the painting is the prompter, who stands among the actors with the book of the play in one hand and a stick in the other. The great importance of the prompter was due to the fact that there was only one complete copy of the play (in manuscript). The actors were given their own lines to learn, but they had no idea of the rest of the play, so it was necessary for the prompter to indicate, by

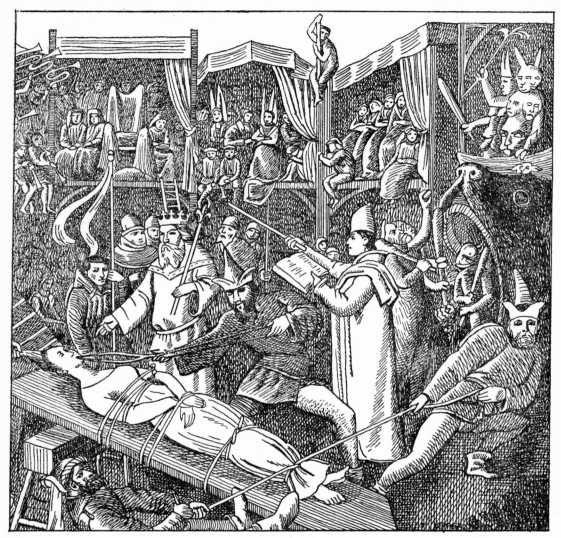

DETAIL REDRAWN FROM THE FOUQUET MINIATURE, WHICH REPRESENTS THE
MARTYRDOM OF ST APOLLONIA

pointing his stick, the actor whose turn it was to speak. The open space in the middle of the market-place was used for various scenes, being very useful, as it could represent any particular place for which there was no setting. It would also be used in conjunction with one of the set stages. In the Fouquet miniature the king has left his throne on one of the stages, descended the steps to the ground, and joined the group of actors in the centre. As much more movement was possible by the use of this central space, so a further development had been made in the history of the theatre. The foundations of many of the Elizabethan stage conventions were laid in the Middle Ages, and it becomes easier to understand how Elizabethan audiences could imagine the place at which the scene was laid without the visual aid of scenery when we realise that it was done in the miracle plays.

In England the miracle plays did not develop in the same way as they did on the Continent.

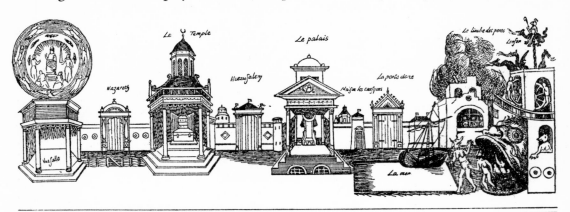

THE SETTING FOR A MYSTERY PLAY IN FRANCE IN THE SIXTEENTH CENTURY

Instead of having set stages round the market-place the scenes were built on wagons. A contemporary description reads:

> . . . a highe place made like a howse with ij rowmes, being open on yᵉ tope: the lower rowme they apparrelled and dressed them selves; and in the higher rowme they played: and they stood vpon 6 wheeles.

Of their progress we are told:

> They first beganne at yᵉ Abbaye gates; & when the firste pagiente was played at yᵉ Abbaye gates, then it was wheeled from thence to the pentice at yᵉ highe crosse before yᵉ Mayor; and before that was donne, the seconde came, and yᵉ firste wente in-to the watergate streete, and from thence vnto yᵉ Bridge-streete, and soe all, one after an other, tell all yᵉ pagiantes weare played.

Something of this arrangement still survives in London in the Lord Mayor's Show, although the 'pageants' are only tableaux, and there is no acting or dialogue.

One of the most popular scenes of the miracle plays was the Hell Mouth, with its assortment of demons, who rushed about making horrible noises, carrying fireworks, and flaming spars on which was thrown powdered resinous pitch, causing clouds of smoke and flame. The demons appeared in most of the scenes, and as they had no lines to speak there must have been great competition for these parts. One rather suspects that the apprentices, being younger and more agile, took most of these devil parts, and when they came into contact with the older citizens (perhaps their masters) no doubt their devilry was most realistic. The Hell Mouth was usually provided with some device for opening, in order to render the effect of fire and smoke belching forth. Although the plays were based on incidents from the Bible, a good deal of comic by-play crept in. Apart from the devils, such characters as the shepherds would probably have a short interlude before the appearance of the angel, in which some invented 'business' could be introduced, possibly some low humour which would have immediate response from the audience. The playing of saints and other sacred

MASKS WORN BY THE DEVILS IN MIRACLE PLAYS

figures, on the other hand, called for no such relation with life, and the acting resolved itself into a series of formal and stilted movements.

In England all the acting of both male and female characters was undertaken by men or boys, a convention that was to last right up to Restoration days. On the Continent, however, women took part in the miracle plays from time to time, and at Metz in 1468 a young amateur actress appeared as St Catherine, and had a large number of lines to speak. The players had to be ready by 4.30 A.M., and as the whole cycle of plays lasted two or three days, they must have found it a very fatiguing business, especially as they had to repeat their performance at every stop on the route. On the Continent, where the plays took place in the market square, they were more fortunate in being able to join the rest of the audience in watching the other scenes when their own performance was over.

Together with the miracle plays, the morality play developed in the later years of the Middle Ages. The morality play had one central figure representing man, and all the abstract qualities of vice and virtue were characterized as real persons. Being more ethical than religious in theme, the morality play was a further step away from the Church's influence in the drama. The staging was similar to that of the miracle plays, but fewer scenes were used. *Everyman* is the best-known example of the morality plays that have survived. In Cornwall there were certain amphitheatres set up in the country where morality plays were performed. There are records of a play called *The Castle of Perseverance* being performed during the reign of Henry VI, in which it is mentioned that Mercy was dressed in white, Ruthlessness all in red, Truth in a sad green, and Peace all in black.

During the fifteenth century the professional actor began to make his appearance again.

It is quite possible that the professional wandering entertainer occasionally played in the miracles. The cycles took so long to perform that interludes of pure entertainment would have been welcome to both players and audience, and no doubt professional advice in acting was frequently sought and given.

## The Renaissance

The fifteenth century saw a great change in social life in Europe, which was reflected in the treatment of the miracle plays. Pageantry became more and more important, and the spoken drama consequently declined. The performances more often took place in the banqueting hall than in the market-place. With the invention of printing, the renaissance of learning, and the many colleges and educational centres that were being founded, the ruling class became more dominant in the lives of the people. Gradually the miracle plays declined in popularity, and drama rediscovered its old form. Scholars began writing plays, using for subject matter much of what they had read in the classic Roman writers.

Italy was the centre of the Renaissance, and there, at the famous academies of Vicenza, Mantua, Milan, Naples, Florence, and Venice, new theatres were built, chiefly for the private performances of plays written by their scholars. Great artists, such as Raphael, designed the theatres and scenery, setting standards which have not been surpassed in the theatres of the whole world. A manuscript by Vitruvius, a Roman architect of the first century B.C., which gave information about architecture in general and the architecture of the Greek theatre in particular, came to light, and the architects of the Renaissance modelled their work on the ancient classic principles expounded in this manuscript. Perspective was one of the fascinating discoveries of the Renaissance, artists and architects (in those days there was very little difference between the two) vying with each other in producing stage settings in which painted perspective was employed to the full. Serlio produced a work of his own on theatre architecture early in the sixteenth century, based very closely on Vitruvius' work. From Serlio we have illustrations showing the principles of stage setting for tragedy, comedy, and pastoral drama, in which trinity all plays of that time could be placed. The scene for tragedy was a street of grand palaces, with a dignified archway in the background and many statues and architectural adornments associated with grandeur. Comedy had an everyday street scene, with an inn, shops, and many balconied windows, at greatly varying levels. It was essentially a lively and human setting, and much closer to reality than was the tragic scene. The pastoral scene emphasized the lyrical qualities. It was a landscape with trees in the foreground and a rocky path wandering between labourers' cottages, such as could be seen anywhere in Italy. Serlio's and other published works on the theatre eventually found their way to England, and formed the basis of stage design in the seventeenth century, when Inigo Jones was designing the scenery for the Court masques.

By the sixteenth century the miracle plays had fallen into disuse, except in a few isolated instances, but companies of professional players were being formed which gave performances of the Interludes, as they were called, in halls and inns. The Interludes were short comic pieces based on everyday life, and were more like our variety sketches than plays, but they certainly proved acceptable to the people of those times.

THE TRAGIC SCENE, AFTER SERLIO

THE COMIC SCENE, AFTER SERLIO

As printing became more universal, scholars in England were busy studying the ancient works and writing plays based on classical principles. The first plays by the scholar play-wrights were performed at the universities, and as they were written without any practical knowledge of the theatre, they seem to us stilted and pedantic. It was left to Shakespeare to infuse that profound knowledge of life, together with practical stagecraft, into the poetry of English drama by producing plays which have remained, and will remain, models for all time.

# CHAPTER THREE
## The Elizabethans

*Plate III*

---

*An Elizabethan Stage*

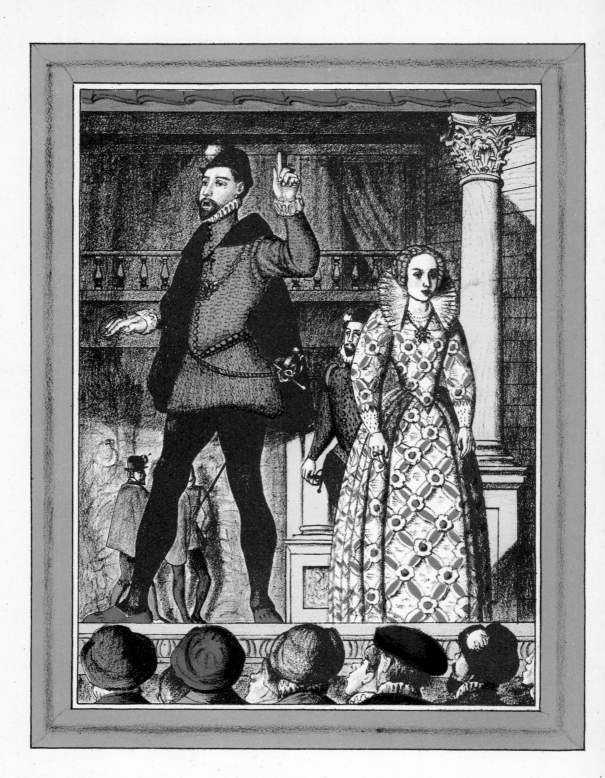

# CHAPTER THREE

# THE ELIZABETHANS

FROM ABOUT THE MIDDLE OF THE SIXTEENTH CENTURY the com-
panies of players which were now well established began to give their performances
on stages set up in the courtyards of certain inns in London. In those days these inns
were large and important establishments, being used as stations in the great network of
carriers who were plying their trade over the whole country. When travel was necessary,
or when goods were dispatched into the country, the inn was inevitably the starting-place.
Horses were hired, goods were transferred from carrier to carrier, and there was much
bustle and excitement. In the early days the actors had to take turns with the carriers in the
use of the courtyard, but later, when the performances attracted large audiences, the proprietors of certain inns gave up the business with the carriers and concentrated on the drama.

The inns were generally of a standard design, the building being in four sections round a
rectangular courtyard, with entrances at the back and front for the wagons and horses. The
courtyard was open to the sky, and round it, on the walls of the inn, were constructed at
different levels two or three galleries, which were roofed over but open at the sides. The
stage would be set up at one end of the courtyard, near the stairs which gave access to the
galleries. At the back of the stage there would probably be a curtain, behind which space
would be provided for the actors to use as a dressing-room. The gallery immediately above
the stage would sometimes be used in the action of the play, and was generally reserved for
the actors. These courtyards could comfortably hold some three or four hundred of the
common people, who would pay a penny or twopence to stand and watch the performance.
The nobility and people of quality, who were also attracted to these inn-yard plays, would

take their seats in the galleries. Often in certain parts of the courtyard a simple platform, or ramp, would be constructed giving a better view of the stage, and possibly a seat would be provided on payment of a further sum. The innkeepers reaped quite a harvest in providing refreshment to the audience, and as they retained the admission fees to the galleries, the actors had to rely on what the courtyard provided them. In some towns the innkeeper was quite an important person; Davenant's father, for instance, at Oxford, was an alderman, and eventually became Mayor of the city. In London, however, they were not so important or highly respected, or they might have helped to mitigate the growing hostility of the City fathers towards the players.

All through the history of the theatre actors have had to contend with prejudice and hostility from either the civic authorities or the Puritans. The charges of the Puritans against the stage and the players were the old charges of the early Christians—ungodliness, idolatry, lewdness, profanity, and evil practices; in brief, that the players were pretending to be what they were not in real life. There was also the eternal complaint of Sunday performances. The charges of the City Corporation were more practical ones. They complained that the public performance of a play was an opportunity for idle apprentices, who met with the sole purpose of creating disorders, and that it was an "unthrifty waste of money of the poor"; they made much also of the accidents that occasionally happened on the stage or among the audience: "sundry slaughters and maimings of the Queen's subjects have happened by ruins of scaffolds, frames, and stages, and by engines, weapons, and powder used in plays."

About 1570 the Lord Mayor and the Corporation were also Puritans, so the players suffered under a double attack. The Lord Mayor would have stopped all performances of plays had not the players foreseen this danger years ago, when in forming their companies they had placed themselves under noble patronage and called their company after the name of their patron; thus we have the Earl of Leicester's Men, the Queen's Men, the Admiral's Men, and so on. Attempts by the City to regulate the players were therefore often interfered with by higher authority, usually through the Privy Council. There was one circumstance, however, in which the City fathers had their way in stopping the performances, and that was in time of great plague. In a hot summer the open sewers and conduits that ran in the streets would do their deadly work, and as the plague was most infectious, all public gatherings would be prohibited. In these times the players would take to the road and tour the country. From 1573 to 1587 there were twenty-three visiting companies giving performances in Stratford, so that Shakespeare must have seen plenty of acting in his youth. The companies also gave private performances at Court, in noble households, at the universities, and at the Inner Temple. They had a universal appeal to all classes of the community, and it is interesting to see how Shakespeare includes in his plays character and episodes especially written for the scholar, the courtier, the poet, and the common people.

In 1576 the players had been having a bad time, what with the plague and the City fathers, so the leading player of the Earl of Leicester's Men launched out with spirit and shrewdness. James Burbage, a carpenter turned player, decided to build a public theatre for plays just outside the City limits, at Shoreditch. This region was rural in those days, and there had

AN ELIZABETHAN PLAYHOUSE

been a pleasure ground (Moorfields) near by, which had been set aside for sports and picnics. It was close enough to the City to attract an audience, and had the great advantage of being outside the jurisdiction of the Corporation. There is little information about the " Theatre," as it was called, but we can imagine it did not differ greatly from later theatres concerning which we are better informed. It was a wooden structure, and probably circular in plan. The Earl of Leicester's Men found their new home very successful, and crowds flocked to their performances. The same year another theatre was built quite near, and called the Curtain, and this also came under the astute Burbage's management.

When, in his early twenties, Shakespeare first came to London he went to live at Shoreditch, and was soon at work at one or other of the two theatres. In 1596 another theatre, the Blackfriars, was opened in the City, which, although it was within the City limits, was outside the jurisdiction of the Corporation, being Crown property. It was part of the old abbey of the Black Friars, which had become Crown property after the Reformation. Other theatres built outside the City limits, on the south bank of the Thames, were the Rose, built in 1587, and the Swan, built in 1595.

There exists a rough sketch of the Swan, made by a visiting Dutchman, Johan de Witt. It shows that the designers of the early theatres compromised between the rectangular inn-yard with its galleries and the circular arenas used for bull-baiting, a popular amusement of the time. The stage was square in shape, and projected well into the arena or pit. The rear part of the stage was roofed over either with tiles or with thatch, and at least one gallery was provided at the rear of the stage for use in staging the plays. There was a central opening in the rear wall with a curtained alcove or inner stage, and on either side a large door. Above the roof of the stage was a small hut or turret, which may have housed some primitive machinery for the stage. From the turret a trumpeter blew his warning blasts announcing the commencement of the performance. A flag also flew from it, and could be seen from across the river, indicating that a performance would be given that afternoon. Around the roofless arena were covered galleries, very much as in the old inn-yards.

On the death of James Burbage his two sons, Richard and Cuthbert, carried on at the Theatre, but owing to some difficulty about the renewal of the lease by the ground landlord they decided to move elsewhere. In 1598 they formed a syndicate with some of the Lord Chamberlain's Men who were playing at the Curtain. The players were Shakespeare, John Heming, Augustine Phillips, Thomas Pope, and William Kemp. At the end of the year, with carpenters and labourers, they began pulling down the Theatre for the timber and fittings, which were to be used, for financial reasons, in building the new theatre. This was called the Globe, and was built, in accordance with the latest stage developments, on the south bank of the river, at Bankside. By this time Shakespeare had written about twelve of his plays, including *Romeo and Juliet*, *A Midsummer Night's Dream*, *The Merchant of Venice*, and *Henry IV*, and he was already acknowledged as the greatest living dramatist. But the Globe was yet to witness the full flower of his genius in the great tragedies he later wrote. The company contained the leading actors of the day, and the Globe outshone all other theatres in the standard of its plays and the quality of the productions. Five years later, when James I came to the throne, he was so pleased with the Globe company that he allowed them to call themselves the King's Men. Their success was further assured when they acquired the Blackfriars theatre, in the City, for use as winter quarters, as this theatre was entirely roofed in, and with a few braziers of burning coal distributed about the house would be reasonably comfortable for cold winter afternoons. Indeed, the company played as often at the Blackfriars as at the Globe, for the Blackfriars was a semi-private theatre and attracted a better class of audience. This was naturally more profitable to the company, as charges could be raised, with a resulting increase in the takings.

The near-by Rose theatre suffered greatly from the competition of the Globe, and so the managers, Henslowe and Alleyn, decided to build a new theatre, which they called the Fortune, in the City, between Golden Lane and Whitecross Street. Although it was a square building instead of being circular like the Globe, its stage was identical, the dimensions being recorded as forty-three feet wide by twenty-eight feet deep. To give some idea of the real size of this stage, it is worth mentioning that the average theatre in London to-day has a proscenium opening of about thirty feet. The stages in those days were well supplied with trap-doors, used not only in the action of certain plays, such as the grave-diggers' scene in *Hamlet*, but also for passing small pieces of scenery or furniture on to the stage. This would be done in full view of the audience, but at the time there would be some action on another part of the stage which would distract their attention. Shakespeare's plays were not split up into separate scenes as they are usually played to-day, but were played with a continuous flow of characters coming on and going off the stage. Often certain characters in a scene would be still speaking when players in the following scene were already in view and approaching another part of the vast stage. The changing atmosphere of successive scenes, from comedy to tragedy, or from the bustle of the public square to the more intimate interior, was created almost entirely by dialogue. When a definite break was required it was effected by a dance or procession, or by the use of rhyming couplets, a stage convention that existed well into the eighteenth century.

The study of *Hamlet* gives much information about the acting and staging of plays in these times. It is possible by reading the play to reconstruct the way in which it was staged. For example, in Act I, scene iv, Hamlet confronts the ghost of his father. This takes place, as Hamlet says earlier, on "the platform," otherwise the gallery above the stage. The Ghost appears and does not speak, but, beckoning Hamlet to follow, makes an exit. Hamlet does so, in spite of protestations from his friends, Horatio and Marcellus. After Hamlet goes they have six lines of dialogue, which gives the Ghost and Hamlet just sufficient time to descend the stairs on to the main stage, where they make their entrance and the Ghost begins to speak. After the Ghost has made his long speech he makes an exit, presumably through a trap-door (the old convention was that ghosts were subterranean beings). Horatio and Marcellus then make their entrance, and, after some conversation with Hamlet, are made to swear secrecy as regards the night's happenings. The Ghost echoes the order to swear; as the stage directions read, " Ghost cries under the stage." When the play is read with all the facilities of the Elizabethan stage in mind some idea of the continual flow of movement is gained. On a modern stage it does not seem so convincing, and some change of setting, such as a drop-curtain, is usually necessary between the two scenes.

Hamlet's directions to the players in Act III, scene ii, are also very illuminating, as they give us Shakespeare's own ideas about acting, which can be summed up as " be natural but not too natural."

Speak the speech, I pray you, as I pronounced it to you, trippingly on the tongue : but if you mouth it, as many of your players do, I had as lief the town-crier spoke my lines. Nor do not saw the air too much with your hand, thus, but use all gently; for in the very torrent, tempest, and, as I may say, the whirlwind of passion, you must acquire and beget a temperance that may give it smoothness. O! it offends me to the soul to hear a robustious periwig-pated fellow tear a passion to tatters, to very rags, to split the ears of the groundlings, who for the most part are capable of nothing but inexplicable dumb-shows and noise. . . . Be not too tame neither, but let your own discretion be your tutor : suit the action to the word, the word to the action; with this special observance, that you o'erstep not the modesty of nature : for anything so overdone is from the purpose of playing, whose end, both at the first and now, was and is, to hold, as 'twere, the mirror up to nature; to show virtue her own feature, scorn her own image, and the very age and body of the time his form and pressure. Now this overdone, or come tardy off, though it make the unskilful laugh, cannot but make the judicious grieve; the censure of the which one must in your allowance o'erweigh a whole theatre of others. O! there be players that I have seen play, and heard others praise, and that highly, not to speak it profanely, that, neither having the accent of Christians nor the gait of Christian, pagan, nor man, have so strutted and bellowed that I have thought some of nature's journeymen had made men and not made them well, they imitated humanity so abominably.

. . . And let those that play your clowns speak no more than is set down for them [probably a dig at Will Kemp, whose habit of introducing his own gags on the stage must have caused Shakespeare a deal of annoyance]; for there be of them that will themselves laugh, to set on some quantity of barren spectators to laugh too ; though, in the mean time, some necessary question of the play be then to be considered; that's villanous, and shows a most pitiful ambition in the fool that uses it.

The players at the Globe were capable of delivering Shakespeare's lines with great speed and zest, and with the constant stream of characters coming and going, they would complete their performance of the play within two hours. The company was organized on a profit-sharing basis. The original syndicate of the two Burbages and the five leading actors were known as the " House-keepers," and received a certain proportion of the takings. The rest of the company received their shares of the receipts according to their status in the company. When these actors became more important, by virtue of their increasing skill, they were promoted to be house-keepers, receiving a further share in the receipts.

To the Elizabethan audiences Shakespeare brought real life, not only in his presentation on the stage of such characters as Sir John Falstaff and Mistress Quickly and the atmosphere of the tavern and the city street, but even in his verse, which had the familiar ring of the town and countryside. It is only necessary to read the works of dramatists immediately prior to Shakespeare to realize the contrast he afforded. They were primarily scholars and literary men, and their verse seems dry, pedantic, and lifeless. They resented the fact that Shakespeare, a common actor, could also write successful plays. Lyly, who was born ten years before Shakespeare, wrote several plays inspired by the classics, developing a prose style made up of puns and the fashionable jugglery of words. Peele, Lodge, Nash, and Kyd, whose *Spanish Tragedy* was one of the most popular plays of the time, all wrote plays modelled on the words of the Roman dramatist Seneca. Robert Greene has become chiefly famous for his attack on Shakespeare; in the publication of one of his plays he advised his university friends to give up writing plays because the actors had " one, an upstart crow, of their own to supply their needs." Even Marlowe, though he wrote some fine poetry, wrote plays that were difficult to act and bring to life. Shakespeare, with his feet firmly planted on the stage and with his acute powers of observation, re-created in dramatic form life in England as he saw it. It was politic, of course, to make the action of the plays take place in some foreign country and to give the important personages, the nobles and princes, foreign names, so that there could be no chance of recrimination by some lord who thought he saw himself caricatured on the stage. But even in the mythical country of Illyria (*Twelfth Night*) he cannot avoid placing the famous tavern of South London, the Elephant, and near Athens (*A Midsummer Night's Dream*) he introduces a group of rustics who are given uncommon but typically English names, and who behave exactly as Shakespeare may have seen them behave in the fields and hamlets of Warwickshire.

Among Shakespeare's contemporary dramatists, his immediate friends were Ben Jonson, Beaumont, and Fletcher. Jonson was continually in trouble, for he was hot-headed and quarrelsome, but he was a fine scholar and wrote some good comedies. Shakespeare's company gave Jonson his first success, putting on *Every Man in his Humour* in 1598. Jonson was in prison three times for various reasons; he was rather overbearing, and at times, no doubt, patronized Shakespeare for his lack of classical learning, although he was always envious of his success. He was honest enough to admit Shakespeare's greatness, however, and when in 1616 the latter died he wrote a sincere memorial in verse. Beaumont and Fletcher, who worked and lived together, were prolific writers and produced over fifty plays between them. They wrote romantic comedies, pastorals, tragedies, and the new kind of play, a tragi-comedy, which had some tragic incidents but a happy ending. Shakespeare's other contemporaries were Dekker, Webster, Ford, Massinger, Marston, and Chapman. Dekker wrote some good comedies, and, understanding the new realism that Shakespeare was achieving, he introduced in his plays many scenes from the low life of the times. Webster and Ford wrote tragedies, Webster's most popular play being *The Duchess of Malfi*.

Shakespeare had a certain limitation in the writing of his plays, in that all the female parts had to be played by boys or men. Women had never achieved any importance in the theatre of the past. The theatre was an essentially masculine domain, and while women did appear in the Roman theatres, it was chiefly in the rôle of singer or dancer. The female parts in the old plays had always been acted by men. Women were very much in the background in the everyday life of Elizabethan times, and not until Restoration days was it considered possible for them to act. Now here was a practical stage problem which Shakespeare solved very well. A boy could easily put on a woman's costume, and, with the necessary make-up and decoration, would pass as a woman. Being a mere boy, however, he would hardly have

D

sufficient experience of life to do justice to the interpretation of the rôle. Shakespeare therefore arranged for the most difficult acting to be done by the male characters. Typical of this procedure is the opening scene of *Twelfth Night*, when the Duke Orsino discusses his mistress at length, so that when she finally appears her character has already been established in the minds of the audience. Another useful device was that of making his heroines assume male attire. When one considers the dress of the time it will be seen that a youth with a slight figure could easily give a very convincing interpretation of a woman in man's costume. In the men's costume the padded doublet and the full breeches or trunk hose would quite conceal a feminine figure, and, conversely, the women's costume, with its enormous skirts and padded sleeves, would easily conceal a boy's figure. The boy players were thoroughly expert at female impersonation, and some of them continued with their feminine rôles even after their voices broke. The part of Lady Macbeth would probably be played by one of these 'senior' boys, who would naturally be much more experienced, and capable of playing a more difficult part.

Apart from the boys who served an apprenticeship with the regular companies there were two troupes entirely composed of boy actors. That they were extremely popular in London is proved by the serious rivalry that they created with Shakespeare's company at one time, as is shown by Hamlet's discussion with Rosencrantz, which concludes:

> HAMLET. Do the boys carry it away?
> ROSENCRANTZ. Ay, that they do, my lord; Hercules and his load too.

" Hercules and his load " is a reference to the Globe, which had a sign outside its entrance of Hercules holding up the world. The companies of boy actors were the choir-boys of St Paul's, who played near the Cathedral, and the choir-boys of the Chapel Royal, who played at the Blackfriars theatre before the Globe company finally acquired it. Ben Jonson wrote plays for the Chapel Royal boys, while Marston and Dekker wrote for the boys of St Paul's. There was great rivalry between Jonson on the one hand and Marston and Dekker on the other, and they attacked each other in successive plays. The popularity of these companies did not last, however, and the public soon deserted them for the regular companies.

Shakespeare himself played various parts in his plays, including the Ghost in *Hamlet* and Theseus in *A Midsummer Night's Dream*, parts that had little personal character, but needed a dignified and poetic interpretation. His chief activity apart from the writing of his plays was in the direction of their production. Some of his chief actors were Richard Burbage, Edward Alleyn, John Heming, who was later to publish his plays, and Will Kemp as leading comic actor. Burbage played all Shakespeare's great tragic parts, and as Shakespeare wrote his plays to suit the actors of his company he must have had Burbage in mind when writing *Hamlet*, *Othello*, *Lear*, and *Macbeth*. Little has been recorded about Burbage, except that his movements were graceful and he was perfectly natural on the stage, while his musical voice gave beauty to quite commonplace verse. Besides playing in Shakespeare's plays he also appeared in many of Ben Jonson's, in Kyd's *Spanish Tragedy*, and in Webster's popular tragedy *The Duchess of Malfi*. Burbage was also a painter, and he has left several portraits of his fellow-actors, which are now in the Dulwich Gallery.

The other great tragic actor of the time was Edward Alleyn. He was noted for his acting in Marlowe's plays, especially in *Tamburlaine*, and he also played in many of Shakespeare's early plays. When Shakespeare was at the Globe Alleyn was in partnership with his father-in-law, Henslowe, first at the Rose and later at the Fortune. He also shared with Henslowe

WILL KEMP

TARLTON, FROM A CONTEMPORARY
MANUSCRIPT

certain interests in bear-baiting, and, being a shrewd man of business, he made a fortune, bought Dulwich manor for £10,000, and founded Dulwich College. Alleyn was a typical example of the Elizabethan, a scholar, poet, courtier, and adventurer, a man with a wide variety of interests, and one always ready to break new ground. He was a very tall man, of splendid physique, and was best in majestic parts.

About 1580 the chief comic actor was Richard Tarlton, whose popularity was probably mainly due to his improvisations. The audience would suggest a theme or verse, to which he would extemporize some doggerel or cap it with another. He was also noted for his jigs, which were humorous dances accompanied by comic patter. The jig usually took place at the end of the play, and was not really connected with it. Tarlton has been associated by many scholars with Hamlet's Yorick. He died in 1588, and Will Kemp took his place as the leading comic actor. Kemp, who modelled his style largely on Tarlton, played with Shakespeare's company and went with them to the Globe. He appeared in many of Shakespeare's early plays, playing Peter (in *Romeo and Juliet*), Dogberry, one of the Dromios, and Launcelot Gobbo. He did not remain long at the Globe, however, possibly because of differences of opinion with Shakespeare, and left to join the Earl of Worcester's Men. He also travelled extensively on the Continent, where he was very popular. He is chiefly noted for his " nine days' wonder "—his wager, which he won, that he would dance all the way to Norwich from London. Other clowns of the time were Robert Wilson, John Singer, and Thomas Pope.

What of the boy actors? There is unfortunately little record of them, although some must have continued playing female parts until they were middle-aged. Nat Field was the most

DETAIL OF COSTUME FROM THE
PORTRAIT OF SIR WALTER
RALEIGH

TYPICAL ELIZABETHAN COSTUME, SHOW-
ING A STUDIED CARELESSNESS IN THE
WEARING OF THE CLOAK

well known, but he graduated from one of the companies of boy players and did not play women's parts with Shakespeare's company. When the Globe company took over the Blackfriars theatre in 1608 they retained the leading boy actors, Ostler, Underwood, and Eggleston, but there is little known about them. No doubt the boys were a constant problem to the companies; they were growing up all the time, their voices would crack, and they would then have to be replaced. Suitable boys must have been scarce, and that is probably why in Shakespeare's plays there are rarely more than two or three female characters.

The costumes worn by the players were most important, as they formed almost the only feature of decoration on the stage. The actors who played nobles and princely characters wore the simple but very richly decorated dress of the period. The fools and clowns wore the costume of the common people. There were certain special costumes not associated with everyday dress. Eastern characters, such as Othello, usually wore a turban of some kind, long, baggy trousers gathered in at the ankle, and a short coat ornamented with the Eliza-

THE ELABORATE COSTUME OF THE COURT
AS WORN BY QUEEN ELIZABETH

COUNTRYWOMAN'S COSTUME

bethan idea of Arabic decoration. Some form of Greek or Roman costume was also used, probably a tight seamless tunic after the style of a cuirass with a short pleated skirt. Buskins and a helmet plentifully decorated with feathers completed the costume, which, as can be seen in old engravings, was in use until the nineteenth century. Robes and gowns were also used for friars and other characters of a special kind. From Henslowe's diary we find that a costume for Cardinal Wolsey cost the company £38 12s. 2d. for " coats, velvets, satins, and lace,"a princely sum in those days. The costumes for the female characters were also expensive, £9 being spent on a taffeta gown, while a skirt of silver camlet cost £2 15s. The women's dress of the period, as worn by the boy players, was very rich in decoration, though simple in shape. The curious stilted shape of the figure was obtained by a leather corset, which had two semicircular side-pieces round the waist, at right-angles to the bodice. The petticoats, and finally the skirt, were drawn in over the side-pieces, which had the effect of bunching out the skirt at the waist, so that it fell in long, straight folds to the ground. It can be seen that the boys could easily manage these rather stiff and all-concealing costumes. The fashionable colour for hair was red (after the false hair of the Queen), and red wigs were naturally very fashionable among the ladies of the Court, another point which gave conviction to the boys' use of them. There was also a great deal of stage jewellery to give the finishing touches to the richness of the costumes. In Shakespeare's plays there is a considerable use of pageantry, and the richness of the costumes played an important part in the many processions and formal dances which punctuated the performances at the Globe and the other theatres. The costumes of the numerous heralds, with their sur-coats emblazoned with heraldic devices, would, with their bold decorative qualities, help to achieve a dramatic and pleasing spectacle. It can well be imagined that costumes were the big expense to the Elizabethan actors, and they generally spent a considerable proportion of the takings in providing additions to their wardrobe.

Music also played a big part in the productions. Shakespeare's innumerable songs and the stage directions in *The Tempest*, for example, called for some small orchestra. In de Witt's sketch of the Swan the word 'orchestra' is written under the first gallery at the left side of the stage, which would be a very suitable place for it. At the end of the various acts a formal dance would be given, in which all the players took part. Music and a flourish of trumpets also accompanied the many processions which are mentioned in the stage directions of Shakespeare's plays. If anyone was killed on the stage a procession was formed to bear off the body, and, no doubt, there was considerable stage business not mentioned in the plays.

Artificial lighting was first used in Shakespeare's time. Although the Globe was open to the sky and performances were given only on summer afternoons, the stage balcony would be in shadow, and in some scenes candlelight could be used for effect. In *Romeo and Juliet* the balcony became Juliet's bedchamber, and would probably have some lighted candles to denote that the action was taking place at night. And in the first scene in *Hamlet*, which, we presume, took place on the balcony, there is Horatio's reference to " the morn, in russet mantle clad, walks o'er the dew of yon high eastern hill," which might indicate the use of a concealed lighting effect, which the Italians were using before this time. The Blackfriars theatre was roofed in, and so artificial lighting was necessary. Probably chandeliers holding numerous candles were the chief source, as they must have been at the performances held at Court.

The development of Shakespeare's art and the Elizabethan theatre was bound up with the growth of Court influence in the drama. Henry VIII was very fond of pageants, masques, and dramatic diversions, and when Elizabeth came to the throne she likewise developed a taste for plays. Shakespeare's company continually played at Court, and the patronage the players enjoyed from various nobles saved them many times from extinction at the hands of the City fathers. Some of Shakespeare's plays are said to have been written to the order of the Queen, and there is an old tradition that *The Merry Wives of Windsor* was the outcome of her wish to see Falstaff in love. There is no doubt that it is not of the same quality as the other plays in which the immortal Sir John appears, and we can guess what Shakespeare thought of it.

When James I came to the throne he was delighted with the players from the Globe, and thenceforth they became the King's Men. As the performances at Court increased it became apparent that the needs of the Court were rather different from the demands of the public audiences. The public wanted plenty of dramatic action, passionate acting, and low-comedy relief, while the Court audiences wanted a more poetic spectacle in which the ladies and gentlemen of the Court could also take part. There is a hint of this in one of Shakespeare's last plays, *The Tempest*, in which Prospero conjures up a masque to celebrate the betrothal of Miranda and Ferdinand. It is suggested by many that Shakespeare was influenced by the masques that were specially written and produced for the Court. Some years before 1611, when it is presumed that *The Tempest* was written, in a masque by Samuel Daniel, Ceres and Juno appear. Nymphs called naiads and reapers performing a country dance appear in other masques which Shakespeare, with his connexions at Court, may have seen. Some writers even suggest that Prospero's explanation of the abrupt ending to the masque in *The Tempest*, the dissolving of " the cloud-capp'd towers, the gorgeous palaces," is a direct reference to the scenic devices of Inigo Jones. While the speech has a deeper, philosophical meaning, it is certainly possible that in writing it Shakespeare was influenced by the scenic splendour of the Court masques. Ben Jonson began writing exclusively for the Court performers, and produced a large number of masques, which were a combination

JAMES I AS A BOY

of spectacle, dances, and formal recitation. No great acting was required in the performances, which were, in effect, a dramatization of the courtly qualities of beautiful and dignified appearance, refined speech, and graceful movement. Inigo Jones, artist and architect, produced the masques and designed the scenic backgrounds and the costumes. Jones had studied art in Italy, and he returned with a store of information about the Italian theatres, which by then had developed the art of staging to a great extent, evolving many stage devices for moving the elaborate scenery, coloured lighting, and many other elements of the theatre which we in this country associate with much later times.

A large number of sketches, plans, and diagrams by Inigo Jones survive to this day and give us considerable information about the staging of the masques. Considerable sums were spent, £3000 being recorded as the cost of a masque produced for the Queen. Ingenuity as well as lavishness was displayed in some of the devices for moving scenery, which was usually done in full view of the audience. The movement of the scenery was, indeed, an integral part of the masque. Gods and goddesses were made to appear and vanish at will by clouds which would move across the scene.

This emphasis on setting was a source of irritation to Jonson, and finally resulted in a quarrel with Jones. Jones, however, was in the stronger position and continued to direct the masques, while other writers provided the scripts.

Within the space of fifty years drama had developed from the pedantic, lifeless verse of the scholar-playwrights to the great force of a Shakespearean tragedy, full of deep penetration of character, in a language that reached heights of perfection that have never been approached since. Acting must also have reached its greatest heights, with Burbage its paragon—for what other actor has had a *Hamlet*, an *Othello*, a *Lear*, written for him? While, with the sumptuous settings and costumes, and with Inigo Jones to direct, the masques achieved new heights of artistic endeavour, which, although never reached again, bequeathed to the public theatres a tradition of spectacle that played a large part in the theatres of later centuries.

# CHAPTER FOUR
# The Italian Comedians

*Plate IV*

---

*The Italian Comedians*

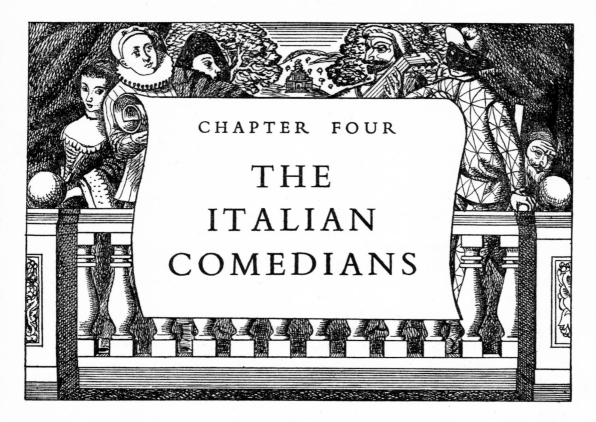

# CHAPTER FOUR

# THE ITALIAN COMEDIANS

WITH THE COMING OF THE RENAISSANCE in Italy and the magnificent theatres that were built to house the spectacular productions of classic plays and opera, there developed quite separately the popular *commedia dell' arte*, or companies of comedians. These comedians developed their art and performances to such a high standard of execution that their work had a strong influence on the development of the theatre in Europe for nearly two hundred years. The entertainment they provided was enjoyed by all classes of the community, and they travelled across Europe with great success, even though they rarely spoke any other than their own tongue. Their success was partly due to the contrast they provided to the regular theatres, which were presenting classic dramas of the past, by drawing the themes and characters of their plays from real life and the people of their own times. They drew largely from observation, playing on the weaknesses and vanities of human beings. In Italy they would often use the dialect of the district in which they were playing.

All the dialogue of the plays was improvised by the players themselves, and so the acting became highly developed and specialized. Each actor developed the presentation of a particular character, which had its own unique personality, and he usually played in the rôle of that character till the end of his days. Each character had its own canons of behaviour on the stage, and the actors had an extensive repertoire of speeches, cracks, and gags which could be used in any given situation. The speeches were so fashioned that they could be lengthened or compressed according to need. In order to give a performance it was only necessary to put up the scenario, the bare outline of the plot, in the wings before the performance, to serve as a guide to the actors in their comings and goings on the stage. The actors co-operated so closely and understood their rôles so well that the performances went with a swing from the very beginning. This could have been done only by highly practised professional players who were masters of their craft. The players often intermarried, as women also had their part in the companies, and the traditions of their craft were handed down from father to son and from mother to daughter. Thus the company was often a family in the real sense of the word.

The influence of the *commedia dell' arte* was felt chiefly in France, where, after a period of insecurity during which they would be invited to perform by the king or the nobles of the Court, followed by their expulsion by Parliament from Paris, they became firmly established in the seventeenth century. At first they performed in their own language, but later they were able to perform in French, and their performances underwent a change in spirit. The characters became more elegant and witty, and the costumes and presentation were adapted to suit the change of style. The French playwright Molière was greatly influenced by the comedians, and at one time his company shared a theatre with them. In 1680 the existing theatres in Paris were unified by the king, and the Théâtre Français was established and given the monopoly for spoken drama. The Italians were allowed to continue their performances at their theatre, the Hôtel de Bourgogne, but they were limited to pantomime and music, which, however, had always played a great part in their presentations. At the end of the seventeenth century they were again driven out of Paris, having become unpopular with the authorities. They came back in 1716, after which they had many years of popularity. They began to perform plays by French writers, and with the influx of French actors into their companies they finally merged into the native drama. By 1780 there were no longer any Italian comedians at the Théâtre des Italiens, although in their own country certain companies of comedians were playing in the old traditional style until the nineteenth century. Some additional characters, such as Gros-Guillaume, Gaultier Garguille, and Turlupin, were created by the French actors who played in comedies in the Italian style.

The most famous actors of the *commedia dell' arte* were Flaminio Scala, Andreini, Biancolelli, and Riccoboni, all cultured men and distinguished as poets and writers. These actors were probably the original writers of much of the dialogue used by the comedians, which was handed down through generations of players. The most famous company was probably the Gelosi, of which Scala and Andreini were members, as was also Andreini's wife, the lovely Isabella, a cultured, witty, and beautiful woman, who gave her name to the heroines of the plays. The companies often united together and then re-formed into new companies, and it is difficult to keep track of them in their constant travels and waves of popularity and expulsion. They helped to shape the theatre in France, and were finally absorbed by it; thence their influence passed to England with Charles II, who, having spent part of his exile in France, must have often seen them in Paris. No doubt, in common with the people of France, he enjoyed their performances, and found the women players witty, amusing, and

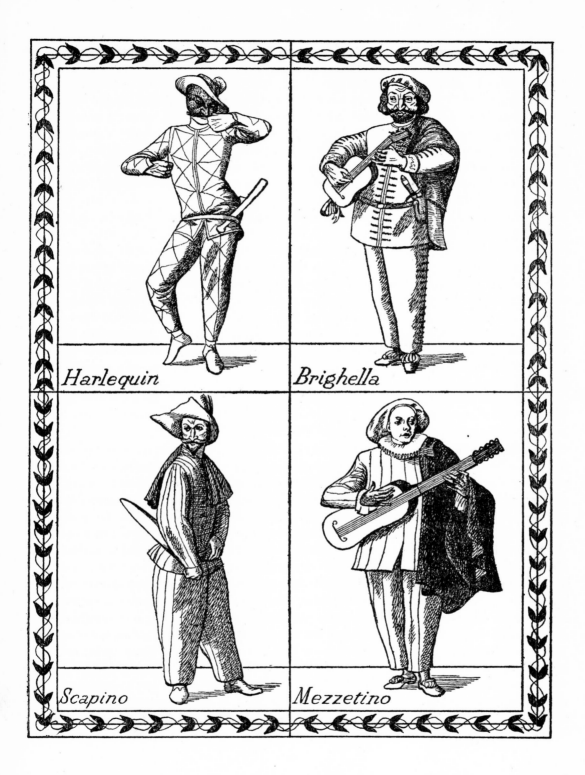

Harlequin

Brighella

Scapino

Mezzetino

beautiful, for after the Restoration he was partly responsible for the acceptance of the actress as a new convention on the English stage.

The Italian comedians had their origins in the dim past of the Roman Atellan theatre, and possibly earlier still. The farces which had become so popular when the Romans had become tired of the Greek tragedies were also improvised from a simple plot or scenario. The pantomime, which developed from the actor having his lines chanted by a chorus while he acted his part in mime, was also to be exploited to great advantage by the Italian comedians. Other links with the ancient classic theatres were the masks worn by the comedians, and the Captain is almost an exact counterpart of a character in a comedy by Plautus. Also, in the early days of the Italian comedians the phallus was worn by Pantalone, and there are numerous other analogies to indicate that the *commedia dell' arte* owed much in its development to the theatre of the past.

The characters of the *commedia dell' arte* were of two main types: the comic characters, who performed the most important parts in the plays, and the 'straight' characters, who provided the love interest, giving a rather poetic or romantic interpretation of their rôles. The characters, being actually created by individual actors, varied with different companies, and adopted various names. Other actors created new characters, which were also handed down through the generations, and altogether there are innumerable characters created by the comedians at various times on their extensive travels. There are, however, certain well-known characters, a description of which will serve to give a picture of the form of the *commedia dell' arte*.

## The Comic Characters

*Arlecchino (Harlequin).* The most famous character of the Italian comedians had originally quite a different personality from the Harlequin who eventually found his way into the English pantomime. He was originally rather a numskull, a valet or servant, a simple native of Bergamo, but although guileless, he was full of pranks and always extremely agile. He would be played by an actor who was also a clever dancer and acrobat, and in many old prints he is seen on stilts, walking on his hands, and generally spending a considerable time in the air. In the seventeenth century a famous Harlequin, called Dominique, or Biancolelli, gave a new interpretation of the character. Harlequin was no longer the rather stupid creature, but became clever and shrewd, and while his character was interpreted almost entirely in mime, he had occasional flashes of brilliant wit. His distinctive costume was originally a simple tunic and breeches with numerous patches, which were supposed to signify his status as a servant. In the seventeenth century the patches became symmetrical diamond shapes of red, blue, and green, separated by yellow or gold braid. He wore a black mask, which had a bristly moustache and sometimes a beard, and at his belt hung his magic sword-bat. He usually wore a skull-cap or a large brimmed hat decorated with a hare's foot, which symbolized his own fleetness of foot. In spite of the changes in the character there has always been something indefinably gay about Harlequin that has captured the imagination of writers, musicians, and artists throughout the centuries, and even to-day, whenever an actor

Pantaloon

the Doctor

the Captain

Scaramouche

in the traditional costume appears on the stage, we anticipate that something wonderfully exciting and amusing will follow.

*Brighella* was also a native of Bergamo, and also a servant, but, unlike Harlequin, he was always wily and clever, and continually busy at some sly mischief. He was a singer, musician, and dancer, always ready to tackle any undertaking, whether it was to serenade his master's mistress or to bait some old man. As soon as his craft and rascality had earned him some money he was content to laze and loaf until necessity forced him once again to engage in some further trickery. He looked ferocious, and indulged in frequent knife-play—provided he was dealing with some one older or weaker than himself. His mask was olive-coloured and had a hooked nose and a moustache and beard. His costume was a short tunic and trousers with green braid trimmings along the seams, a short cloak, and a soft hat with a green border. At his belt he always carried the symbols of his character—the money-pouch and dagger.

*Scapino (Scapin)*, a servant and companion of Brighella, was also always ready to put out his hand for money, but where Brighella would draw his dagger Scapino would make a rapid exit. In common with the other comic characters, he was continually involved in amorous intrigues, both on his own account and on his master's. As a character he was not of the first importance, being actually a variation of Brighella. His costume seems to have varied considerably, but it followed the general tradition of valet costumes in having a small cape with a short tunic and loose trousers. His costume was usually decorated with green and white stripes to indicate that it was some kind of livery.

*Mezzetino (Mezzetin)* was another familiar of Brighella, with similar but milder characteristics. At the end of the seventeenth century his costume was redesigned in France by Constantin, who played the character without a mask. The costume was similar to Scapino's, but with red and white stripes instead of green and white. Mezzetin was a great favourite in the early eighteenth century in France, and appears in many of Watteau's paintings of the comedians.

*Pantalone (Pantaloon)*, the dupe, a respectable citizen of Venice; he is always old and has usually retired from business. Money is his ruling passion, and his avarice constantly brings him trouble. He may have a young wife or a daughter who is continually engaged in some love affair behind his back, and sometimes even before his eyes. Occasionally he would fall in love himself, but always with some young maiden who was an incorrigible flirt and used him for game and the money she extracted from him in return for her favours. His traditional costume was a short red jacket and the tight-fitting trousers to which he has given his name, with a long trailing cloak or gown of black, similar to that worn at one time by the Venetians as a sign of mourning because of the successes of the Turkish pirates. A small brimless cap and slippers (Shakespeare mentions " the lean and slippered pantaloon with spectacles on nose ") and the all-important money-pouch at his belt complete his costume. In some early engravings the phallus is discernible, a relic of the days of the ancient theatre. His mask was brown, with a long hooked nose, grey moustaches, and a short white beard with two absurdly long points.

*The Doctor* was another dupe. He was a product of the university at Bologna and the embodiment of all the foolish, pedantic professors in the world. His knowledge of life was gained from his books, from which, however, he could never quote correctly. His knowledge was profound in letters, medicine, philosophy, astronomy, and the law. He had learnt everything, but of life he understood nothing. He was, of course, continually meddling in other people's affairs and laying down the law, and he naturally provided Harlequin and his fellows with great sport. Like his old friend Pantalone, he was occasionally assailed by the gentler passion, with the result that he was always caught in countless ridiculous situations. His costume was the black dress of the man of science and letters of the time. He originally wore a long black cloak and a small hat, but in the seventeenth century the cloak became shorter, being worn draped over a black tunic, and the hat became enormously large, with a great wide brim. Round his neck he wore a large ruff, and always under his arm or in his hand he carried a book or treatise. His mask was curious in that it covered only his nose and forehead, and was either black or flesh-coloured. He also wore a moustache and a short pointed beard.

PULCINELLA

*The Captain*, the braggart, looked forbidding and ferocious. Armed with a long rapier, he strutted about, twirling his moustaches. He had been away to the wars and performed deeds of prodigious bravery, but, strangely enough, all his victims were alive and well. His long-winded, bombastic talk was, no doubt, fully punctuated with strange oaths acquired in foreign lands. Of course, he was really an abject coward, and Harlequin and his fellows had only to make the clinking noise of men-at-arms off-stage for the Captain to collapse with fright on the stage and pretend to be dead. A very famous Captain was Francesco Andreini, who played with the Gelosi troupe in Paris. He had been a soldier himself, and was for a time a prisoner of the Turks; no doubt, therefore, in his interpretation of the character he drew on his own experiences. The Captain was originally, like his fellows, a native of Italy, but later, in the seventeenth century, when Spain was dominating the rest of Europe, he became a Spaniard. His costume followed the military dress of the times, and changed with each successive period. In the early seventeenth century he wore tight-fitting clothes, decorated with stripes, a plumed felt hat, and, usually, the high boots of the time. His mask was flesh-coloured, with a large hooked nose and great bristling moustaches. One of his most important properties was his great sword, which was never unsheathed, but was worn with the point thrust aggressively upward.

*Scaramouche* was originally a variation of the Captain, but of much lighter calibre. He was more adroit and less bombastic, and was something of a musician and dancer. He appeared in a completely black costume, and as played by Fiorillo in the seventeenth century he wore no mask. In common with the valets, he was continually involved in picking pockets and dodging blows. Like the Captain, he bragged of his imaginary feats of prowess to impress the ladies and to scare peaceful citizens.

*Pulcinella* or *Policinella* (*Punchinello*), from whom has evolved our own English Punch.

PEDROLINO

A LOVER

He is considered by many scholars to be a direct descendant of a Roman comic character known as Maccus, and some ancient statuettes which have been unearthed have similar characteristics, including the great hooked nose and round belly. The hunchback is a more recent development. Pulcinella usually appeared as an old bachelor, was sensual and cruel, but possessed a sense of humour and showed constant flashes of wit. His costume, based on the traditional dress of the peasants of Italy, was white in colour. The costume, with those of the other characters, changed in France in the seventeenth century to red breeches and a green trimmed jacket. He wore a ruff and a tall conical hat, or sometimes a skull-cap. His mask was chiefly all nose, though it was sometimes adorned with a moustache and beard.

*Pedrolino* (*Gilles*, *Pierrot*). Another valet, but this time a trustworthy one. He was a rather simple character, and when encouraged by Harlequin to engage in trickery he was invariably the only one to be caught and punished. He was originally closely related to Pulcinella and

Brighella, but in France he developed into a more attractive and elegant personality. His costume was the simple white tunic, loose trousers with a large ruff, and a soft felt cap. In the eighteenth century he developed large buttons on his tunic and long sleeves that concealed

SEVENTEENTH-CENTURY STAGE COSTUME
AS IT MIGHT HAVE BEEN WORN
BY THE SOUBRETTE

SEVENTEENTH-CENTURY STAGE COSTUME
AS IT MIGHT HAVE BEEN WORN
BY THE INAMORATA

his hands, and he also acquired a strange quality of sadness. He was played without a mask, the actor's face usually being powdered white.

## The 'Straight' Characters

*The Lovers (Men)* were known by various names, such as Fabio, Ottavio, Silvio, Leandro, Lelio, and Flavio. Their only characteristic was that of being in love and of serving as a foil

E

63

to the comic characters. They were always good-looking and elegant, and were dressed as young gallants of the time. The actor had to interpret the part in a poetic and cultured manner, and he appeared just a trifle ridiculous. The Lovers (or Inamoratos) were usually played by men of birth and position. Sometimes the noble before whom the actors performed would play the part, and it was often played by the director of the company. The Inamoratos played without a mask, as did the Inamoratas, or women Lovers.

A BALLERINA

*The Inamoratas* were also known by various names, such as Flaminia, Lavinia, Aurelia, and Isabella. Women first appeared on the stage as actresses during the sixteenth century, and in France were welcomed with joy, but in Italy they were not allowed to play in the Papal States until the eighteenth century. Their numerous names came from individual actresses, who had their own particular characteristics. Isabella, the famous wife of Andreini, and the leading actress in the company (the *prima donna*), renowned for her beauty, her cultured wit, and her poetic writings, made of the character an idealized type of a woman in love. Her costume was the elegant dress of the period.

The *Soubrette* (or servant), confidante to the Inamorata, had many names, such as Liletta, Smeraldina, Olivetta, Francheschina, or was known more popularly as Columbine. She was a buxom wench, and was usually in love with one of the valets. She was on close terms with Harlequin, and would willingly enter into the intrigues hatched by him and his companions. She had a ready wit and sometimes some outrageous lines to speak, while she was often required to disguise herself in the costume of a cavalier, a doctor, or even as Harlequin. Originally her costume was that of the common people of the sixteenth century, particularly distinguished by a large white apron, but later in France her dress became indistinguishable from that of her mistress.

The *Ballerinas* and *Canterinas*, the dancers and singers. They could both sing and play several instruments, and sometimes performed acrobatic feats or danced on a tight-rope. Their rôle was to perform in the intervals of the action of the play, and sometimes to sing the story of the play as an epilogue.

The description of the various characters indicates the usual theme of the plays, which was the very ancient one of marital infidelity. Young wives of old men and virtuous daughters of rich merchants would engage in involved and complicated love intrigues. The valets and the servant-maids engineered the innumerable ridiculous situations, while providing secondary love affairs, and there was continual plot and counter-plot. The complete success of the improvisations was due to the style in which these things were done. In addition to being masters of their particular characters and having numerous appropriate speeches at their finger-tips the actors could easily mime their story, thus making it clear to the audience without giving away any information to the other characters. They had also an extensive repertoire of amusing tricks, some acrobatic and some very old and simple but effective bits of stage business. They would make themselves into fountains, or imitate statues, remaining motionless and unseen by other characters until the *dénouement* of the plot required them to resume their own characters. Syringes for the squirting of water, and other properties which to-day we associate with the circus or variety stage, were greatly in use. One can imagine that although the players were never at a loss for words, it would sometimes be effective for them to use some of this byplay as a relief to the spoken parts of their show. The comedians also had stock cues which simplified the entrances and exits of the various characters, thus ensuring smoothness of playing and giving to the performance a sense of dramatic form.

The companies were continually meeting opposition to their performances from either the Church or the civic authorities, and so they had to be continually on the move. They travelled through most countries in Europe, to Austria, Germany, France, Spain, and England, and wherever they performed they left behind ideas which were adopted in the theatres of those countries. A company had been in England as far back as 1527, and in later times Charles II gave them permission to play for a season in London, during which they proved very popular. Shakespeare must have known of them, as he describes Pantaloon in *As You Like It*, while the comic letter scene in *Twelfth Night* might easily have been a scene played by the comedians. Indeed, is there not something of the Captain, Harlequin, Brighella, Columbine, and the Doctor in Sir Toby, Sir Andrew, Fabian, Maria, and Malvolio?

The companies of comedians were constantly on the move, and as they could not expect to find a theatre in every town they visited they usually carried with them a portable stage with curtains in addition to their innumerable properties. In many old prints these portable stages can be seen set up in the market-place. They were usually just simple square platforms with a decorated curtain as background. The characters entered from short ladders at the side. Some of the early troupes were hardly more than mountebanks, and when in a market-place or at a fair combined the sale of medicines, ointments, or ballad sheets with their acting.

By the nature of their art they could adapt themselves easily to whatever setting and scenic possibilities there were available. The Italians were well ahead in stage technique throughout the sixteenth and seventeenth centuries, and we can be sure that the comedians, professionals as they were, had the ability to make full use of scenery and stage machinery wherever it was to be found. They were experienced in the use of coloured lighting, fireworks, and fountains, which provided dramatic and spectacular effects during their performances. The settings were usually of an architectural nature, and would represent a street or market-place in perspective. In France in the seventeenth century the comedians used a great variety of settings, interiors, and outside sets, either architectural or in the form of a pastoral landscape. At the Hôtel de Bourgogne theatre they had a permanent architectural setting, in the centre of which was a large arch, behind which were placed interchangeable back-

THE COMEDIANS ON THE STAGE OF PALLADIO'S THEATRE AT VICENZA

cloths to represent various scenes. When they performed at Palladio's famous classic theatre at Vicenza, in Italy, they had the elaborate permanent setting, with three archways giving perspective views of streets of solidly constructed wooden houses. The characters could be seen in any street, yet, being invisible to each other, several could appear simultaneously and continue with their involved plotting quite naturally. There were two further doorways at the side of the arches, so the actors had plenty of variety in their comings and goings.

CHAPTER FIVE

# The Restoration Theatre

*Plate V*

*The Restoration Theatre*

1660

# THE
# RESTORATION THEATRE

BETWEEN THE YEARS 1642 AND 1660 the theatres were closed and all stage performances prohibited by Parliament, but it would be wrong to assume that when the theatres were finally reopened there was a complete break with the traditions of the past. Apart from spasmodic attempts to reopen the theatres (the play usually being broken up by Parliamentary soldiers) and occasional private performances, most of the players took to the road, and performed at the big fairs held all over the country. In certain parts of the country the new régime was not very welcome, so it is probable that performances went on unchecked in these parts. In 1660, then, there were a large number of players alive and active who had begun their careers in the reign of Charles I, and it was a great man of the theatre of those days, Sir William Davenant, who played the chief part in providing the link with the past.

Sir William Davenant, poet and practised writer for the theatre, was a man of great tact and diplomacy, with a genius for making friends. Although he fought for the King in the Civil War he had friends among the Parliamentarians who were to prove very useful to him. Born in Oxford in 1606, the son of an innkeeper, he was considered by many to be a natural son of Shakespeare, who had often stayed at the inn. His mother was known as a great beauty and a very witty woman, and at all events Davenant had Shakespeare for a godfather. Inheriting his mother's wit, he achieved fame as a poet and dramatist, was knighted by Charles I, and became Poet Laureate. In his early years he lived in noble households and at Court, gaining experience of the high life of the time. Most of his serious plays deal with the

SIR WILLIAM DAVENANT

amorous and political intrigues of the society of palaces, banqueting halls, and council chambers of far-off lands, but no doubt he drew on his own early experiences. Davenant's plays were found morally acceptable, and even Charles I, in going over the text of *The Wits*, allowed certain parts that were struck out by an over-zealous censor.

Inigo Jones, who was producing the Court masques, turned to Davenant for material after quarrelling with Ben Jonson, and Davenant rapidly climbed in Court favour. In 1634 *The Temple of Love*, a masque which was performed at Whitehall for the Queen and her ladies, gained a reputation for him. Three years later Jonson died, and Davenant succeeded him, as the patent awarded by Charles I explains, as poet in the service of the Court. Although this position was not clearly defined, it can be assumed that he was recognized as holding the office of Poet Laureate. His influence with the King became greater, and he was granted a patent to build a theatre in which to present " plays, musical entertainments, scenes, and other like presentments." Davenant proposed to introduce the spectacle and scenery of the Court masques into the public theatres, which were still carrying on the Shakespearean tradition of simplicity of setting. However, with political clouds on the horizon and possibly some disagreement as to the site of the new theatre, it was not erected until over twenty years later.

At the beginning of 1640 Davenant wrote his last masque, in which all the art of Inigo Jones and his assistant John Webb brought to a climax the pride and beauty of Court pageantry. Later in the year Davenant was made manager of a company of players at the Phœnix Theatre (also known as the Cockpit) in Drury Lane, replacing the previous manager, William Beeston, who had presented an unlicensed play containing some topical allusions that gave offence to the King. Beeston had been arrested and the theatre closed down, and the King, knowing of Davenant's wish to have his own theatre, appointed him to " govern, order, and dispose " the players in their plays and productions. The Phœnix was a small theatre, and there was obviously not sufficient room for Davenant to carry out his schemes of painted scenery and elaborate stage machinery. He remained in charge until 1641, when he was forced to flee to the country to avoid being arrested by the Parliamentary soldiers, as at this time he held some position in the royal army. He was apprehended at Faversham and brought to London, where he was detained for two months, then being released and eventually reaching France. He returned, however, in 1642, when he joined the King's forces and remained with them until the defeat of Marston Moor, after which he again escaped to France.

SETTING BY INIGO JONES FOR DAVENANT'S MASQUE "THE TEMPLE OF LOVE"

Ill-luck again dogged him, for while he was sailing to America his ship was captured by a Parliamentary frigate and he was brought to London and confined in the Tower. Tradition has it that Milton finally secured his pardon and ultimate release from imprisonment. In 1652 Davenant found himself a free man, but with no position and practically penniless. No doubt he used his ability and knowledge of the stage in some of the private performances that were surreptitiously given during the period of Puritan rule, and he must certainly have kept in touch with his old friends of the theatre.

At this time there was, among the scholars and writers particularly, a quiet but constant protest at the closing of the theatres, and in 1656 Davenant, using all his tact and political genius, actually approached the Commonwealth Secretary of State, suggesting the value of

MASQUING COSTUME FOR THE KING
DESIGNED BY INIGO JONES

MASQUING COSTUME FOR THE QUEEN
DESIGNED BY INIGO JONES

stage presentations of moral value for political purposes. Although this fell through, in the same year Davenant gave a private performance in a hall at the back of his own house. The play itself was a plea for the opening of the theatres, introducing Aristophanes and Diogenes in the course of the argument, and we can be sure that Aristophanes wins hands down. The success of this venture encouraged Davenant to more ambitious efforts, and there followed

*The Siege of Rhodes*, an opera, so called, with the scenery designed by John Webb. The stage was only eighteen feet wide and nine feet high, and the several scenes were changed by easily movable flats. By simplification Webb successfully applied the ideas and innovations of the masque stage to a more intimate setting. The settings were composed of three sets of wings and a backcloth, which could be easily changed without machinery. The step from a private theatre in Davenant's own house to a public theatre was the next important move, and in 1658 Davenant finally got permission from the authorities to reopen his old theatre, the Phœnix. He obtained the favour of the authorities by including some propaganda in his opening production, which he again called an opera, *The Cruelty of the Spaniards at Peru*, playing on the hatred of Cromwell for Catholic Spain. The opera was merely a series of declamatory speeches, with songs and musical interludes, against a pictorial background of painted scenery. Although only a slight piece, it was the thin end of the wedge, and Davenant, becoming bolder, followed it up with *The Siege of Rhodes*. Owing to the opposition this created, coming on top of his implication in a surreptitious attempt to bring back the new King from exile, Davenant found himself again in prison. He still had some influence in high places, however, and in August 1659 he was again released, performances resuming at the Phœnix early in 1660 without much hindrance. Davenant had sensed the changing political atmosphere, and soon after he left for France to join the royal entourage, returning in triumph the same year a figure of importance, and in a position to carry out his long-cherished ambition of presenting publicly his plays in the way for which he had worked and struggled so many years.

With Davenant in the royal party was Thomas Killigrew, who was attached to the Court of Charles I, and had joined the new King in exile. He had written plays and had them performed in the past, and he had also travelled in France and Italy, and had seen some of the great technical achievements developed there. While in exile he continued to write poetical works of a rather fanciful nature, which were very acceptable to the Court audiences. After the Restoration Killigrew and Davenant were granted a patent by the King giving them the monopoly of dramatic entertainment, which indirectly affected the development of the theatre in this country for nearly two hundred years. They each formed companies, Killigrew's being known as the King's Players and performing at the new Theatre Royal in Drury Lane, and Davenant's as the Duke of York's Players, performing first at a theatre in Salisbury Court, and later in a converted tennis-court at Lincoln's Inn Fields.

For the next few years, however, things did not go smoothly, and the two companies broke up, united, and broke away again. New theatres were built, but there were long periods when they were closed, during the years of plague and the Great Fire. The vicissitudes of management were great and various, but both companies kept on, and when Davenant died, in 1668, the management was carried on by his wife, a shrewd business woman, and later by his son, Charles Davenant, in conjunction with some of the leading actors. Killigrew's company also carried on when he died, with his son Charles as manager.

From the time of the Restoration also certain foreign companies of players performed in London. The Royal Court when in exile in France had developed a taste for French drama, and companies from France frequently performed, and were very popular. Even more popular were the Italian comedians, who came to London at various times, and in 1683 played at Windsor before the King.

The audiences of the new theatres were chiefly composed of people of the Court and gallants of the town, and the new plays had to be written to suit their tastes. The common folk still regarded the theatre as an appurtenance of the Court, and the old Puritan influence was still very strong, few of the stolid middle class ever going to the play. The ladies and gentlemen of the Court were on very close terms with the players, especially the women players, who were now accepted on the stage. Pepys was a very keen playgoer, and from his diary we find that at the end of the play he would go behind the scenes to chat with the players, and perhaps steal a kiss from Nell Gwyn.

The first productions of the two companies were chiefly the old mainstays—Shakespeare, Beaumont and Fletcher, Ben Jonson, and others of their times—but even during the Commonwealth plays had been written and even printed. Adaptations were also made from the French dramatists, including Molière and Corneille. Davenant was too busy at management to do much writing himself, and his works were chiefly adaptations and translations, but he had works by the new dramatists to fall back on, such men as Dryden, Sir Robert Howard and his brothers, and Lord Orrery. Comedy was the vogue, although tragedy and poetical works set in distant lands were also popular.

The young gallants went regularly to the theatres, not only to see but to be seen. The auditorium was illuminated as brightly as the stage itself, and witty conversation and gossip flowed continually in the audience throughout the performance of the play. People would come and go at all times, and sometimes there would be an argument in the pit leading to a duel: it is recorded that during a performance of *Macbeth* a young gallant met his end at the point of a sword. Such were the conditions under which the players performed, and yet they went from strength to strength. The audience also shaped the conditions of writing a successful play—it had to be witty and contain plenty of amusing situations—and the later writers successfully conformed to these requirements. Among the more important of these dramatists were Congreve, Wycherley, Farquhar, and Sir John Vanbrugh. The plays of this time contained plenty of topical allusions, and, no doubt, the performance of the players was partly based on observation of the mannerisms and excesses of the Court audiences. To-day the Restoration comedies still remain witty and amusing, but have a quality of coarseness which in those days was no more than commonplace.

During the Restoration period a great development took place in the staging of plays, and this affected the arrangement of the theatres and the design of the new buildings. At first, of the two companies only Davenant's made wide use of painted scenery and mechanical devices. Killigrew's company kept the traditional simple stage of Shakespeare, and there was some outward rivalry between the two companies on this question. Davenant decided that his present theatre was not big enough to house the scenery he wanted, and so he decided to build a new theatre at Dorset Garden. He died, however, before it was opened. The theatre was designed by Wren and was very elaborate and ornate. The other company had not been doing too well at the Theatre Royal, and a disastrous fire did not help, so that occasionally the two companies would join together and act at the Duke's Theatre,

THE DUKE'S THEATRE, DORSET GARDEN

as the building at Dorset Garden was called. Later they united finally, and played at the new Theatre Royal. Theatre-building after this period differed in many respects, but conformed to certain general principles. The stage projected into the centre of the auditorium, as in Shakespeare's day, but it also went back past the procenium arch to an equal depth. The proscenium, heavy and ornate, had two stage-doors on either side, which were used by the actors, and above these were stage boxes, usually occupied by the audience, but sometimes used in the play for balcony scenes. On one side the stage boxes were reserved for the orchestra, or, as in the Duke's Theatre, a special box was provided at the top of the proscenium arch. Efforts were made to place the orchestra in the pit below the stage, but they met with disapproval from the audience, who liked to have nothing between themselves and the players.

The scenery was composed of flat wings on either side of the stage, which were fixed in slots on the stage, and with backcloths or shutters, all readily movable. There was a curtain behind the proscenium which, when lowered, cut off the scenery from the apron, as that part of the stage in front of the proscenium was called. The curtain rose after the customary prologue and revealed the setting, but it did not descend until the end of the play, and all scene-changing took place in full view of the audience. This was the time when the songs or musical interludes would be given.

Lighting was by lamps and candles, and as far back as 1598 the Italians were using a glass oil-lamp which could be filled with coloured liquid and reflected coloured light. At the Court masques of Charles I coloured lighting had been extensively used, strips of coloured silk being placed in front of the groups of candles and lamps situated behind the scenes. The general lighting came from great circular fittings, which held many candles and were hung above the apron. These also illuminated the auditorium, and there were probably further candles round the boxes and galleries. About the time of the building of the new theatre at Dorset Garden there came into existence an early form of footlights. These consisted of six oil-lamps at the edge of the stage, in the centre, which could be controlled in some way to suit the action of the play. A night scene, for instance, would require some diminution of the lighting, and although the great chandeliers would be kept going, the footlights would be lowered as a concession to reality, and the player would also carry a candle, to help the convention. The development of the theatre of this time paved the way to the modern picture stage, wedding the simple stage of Shakespeare to the wealth of spectacle of the Court masques.

The most famous actor in the Restoration theatre was Thomas Betterton, who dominated the scene until the beginning of the eighteenth century. According to most writers of the time, he was excellent both in tragedy and comedy, and some space devoted here to his life will serve to give a general impression of the way in which the actors of the time lived and worked. There is little information regarding his early life, but he was born in 1635, the son of an under-cook to Charles I. Betterton displayed early tendencies towards reading and study at school, and he was apprenticed as a young man to a bookseller who had some connexions with the stage, having at one time been wardrobe-keeper and prompter at the Blackfriars theatre. With him as an apprentice was Edward Kynaston, who also became a

THE STAGE OF THE DUKE'S THEATRE

well-known actor. The two young men probably started acting during the period of surreptitious private performances, when the theatres were closed. Betterton almost certainly appeared when Davenant decided to reopen the Phœnix after the performances in his own

house. In 1660 Betterton signed a contract with Davenant, which is interesting as it showed the method of payment to actors. The total receipts of the house were divided into fifteen parts or shares, of which three went to the management for the house-rent, the building of scenery, and costumes and properties. Seven went to Davenant for the maintenance of the women players' costumes and his own personal expenses. The other five shares were divided between the actors. Mention is made in the contract of the perpetual maintenance of a private box for Thomas Killigrew, which seems to indicate that although the two companies showed outward rivalry, the two managers were on very good terms.

Betterton played leading parts with Davenant's company. It is as well to mention that a play seldom ran more than a week at a time in those days, and it was quite common for a play to have only one performance, due, no doubt, to the limited audience and the fact that there were only two companies permanently in London. From Pepys we read that

BETTERTON AS HAMLET

in 1661 Betterton played Hamlet: "To the Opera, and there saw 'Hamlet, Prince of Denmarke,' done with scenes very well, but above all, Betterton did the Prince's part beyond imagination." This was the most successful tragedy for the company for many years, both as regards the money taken and the reputation gained. About the same year the company presented another of Davenant's own plays, *Love and Honour*, and in this production we learn of "the King giving Mr Betterton his Coronation Suit in which he acted the part of Prince Alvaro." The Duke of York and Lord Oxford also lent their coronation clothes to the actors. This indicates the close relationship between the players and the audience of those days, and emphasizes the King's special interest in the theatre.

A link with the theatre of Shakespeare comes to light when, in 1664, Betterton played in *Henry VIII*. A writer of the time says, "The part of the King was so right and justly done by Mr Betterton, he being instructed in it by Sir William, who had it from old Mr Lowen, that had his instructions from Mr Shakespeare himself." Mrs Betterton also appeared in this production. The constant presentation of new plays and old revivals being such a strain on the actors, and the time being limited, there could have been few rehearsals. Pepys writes of *The Bondman* in 1664: ". . . it is true for want of practice many of them forgot their parts a little, but Betterton and my poor Ianthe [Mrs Betterton] outdo all the world."

Betterton wrote three plays himself and played in them with his wife; they were successful and had many revivals. In 1671 he moved with the company to the new theatre in Dorset Garden, and with another leading actor, Harris, formed part of the management with Lady Davenant and her son Charles, who was also acting with the company. Betterton continued with success, and in 1684, when the two companies were united, had available also the new plays of Killigrew's company. Betterton's chief qualities as an actor were dignity and sincerity, and he seemed to get really under the skin of a part. Apparently he was able to give an impression of being natural on the stage, thus contrasting favourably with other actors of those days, whose ranting, "tearing a passion to tatters," was so common at the time. In Pepys and other writers of the time mention is continually made of a successor taking Betterton's part in a play and proving always a disappointment to the audience. A description of Betterton gives him

> a great head, a short thick neck, stoop'd in the shoulders, and . . . fat short arms, . . . his left hand frequently lodg'd in his breast, . . . his actions were few, but just. . . . His aspect was serious, venerable, and majestic. . . . His voice was low and grumbling, yet he could tune it by an artful climax which enforc'd universal attention even from the fops and orange girls.

In 1709 he had a famous benefit night. The play was Congreve's *Love for Love*, in which he played Valentine, and there was a great gathering of distinguished people, who overflowed from pit and gallery on to the stage itself.

Betterton appears to have been a man as highly respected for his moral character as for his dramatic powers. He continued playing intermittently up to 1710, when he died. He had many friends among the distinguished people of his day, and he was greatly mourned at his funeral in Westminster Abbey, where he was laid to rest. Some of the other important actors of his time were Mohun, who began his career in the time of Charles I, Kynaston, Harris, and Charles Hart. Mountfort was the leading comic actor, and some of his companions were Haines, Nokes, Doggett, and John Lacy.

As mentioned previously, the introduction of women on the stage was an innovation in this country. On the Continent women had been acting for many years, but in Elizabethan times all the women's parts had been played by boys and young men. Older women's parts were played by the same actors as they grew older. In 1660 a performance of *Othello* by the King's Players had an actress in the cast. The audience were warned in the prologue, and the epilogue made this inquiry, " And how d'ye like her? " The applause that followed ensured the establishment of the actress as a member of the company. One of the first women to appear on the stage was a Mrs Coleman, who appeared in Davenant's production of his opera *The Siege of Rhodes*. Now that women were accepted on the stage, the female parts in the plays could be assured of authentic interpretation, and also a new interest in the theatre was created for the young gallants of Court and town. The most famous of the actresses who graced the Restoration stage was Nell Gwyn, although she played for only a short period, chiefly in comedy parts. Pepys found her a lively and witty creature, although it is probable that she was more important as a personality than as an actress. A great tragic actress of the time was Mrs Barry, who often acted with Betterton. Betterton's wife must also have been a very clever actress to have sustained so many rôles with her husband. In comedy Mrs Mountfort, with her robustness and vivacity, gave ideal interpretations of the parts in the new comedy of manners. The end of the century saw the rise of the celebrated Mrs Bracegirdle, an extremely capable actress. She had the vivacity and attack necessary for delivering the prologues and epilogues, which in those days were written for special performances, and she could sing and dance very well. She also appeared in tragic parts, particularly in a play by Mrs Aphra Behn, who was possibly the first Englishwoman to write for the stage.

It is interesting to note that while vaguely historical costumes were sometimes worn by the male players, the actress always appeared in the dress of the current vogue, with perhaps just a suggestion of another period when necessary for the plot, such as a plumed headdress or some small concession in the details of the costume. Historical accuracy on the stage was not established until well into the nineteenth century, and until then Shakespeare was usually played in modern dress.

Among the institutions of the stage that survived until the nineteenth century were the benefits. Leading players, and later authors, had a benefit performance during the season, for which they received the entire takings, after certain expenses had been deducted. This system rather tended to reduce their regular salaries, though the stars were always well paid.

Another stage convention founded in Restoration days was the 'invisible' candle-snuffer. The tallow candles in those days needed constant attention in order to make them burn brightly. There were usually two attendants who looked after the candles, one on the stage and the other in the auditorium. No matter what was happening on the stage, should a candle begin to splutter the attendant would walk on to the stage, quite unconscious of the actors, and attend to his business; having concluded which, he would make a dignified exit. His appearance on the stage on these occasions was accepted in the same way as the scene-shifters were accepted, as a necessary part of the impedimenta of the stage. Far from decrying the appearance of the candle-snuffer on the stage, at a most dramatic moment, perhaps, members of the audience, on seeing certain lights fail, would actually raise a shout for him, and woe betide if he was not soon forthcoming !

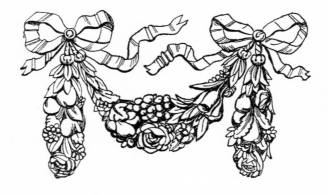

# CHAPTER SIX

## The Eighteenth Century

*Plate VI*

*The Stage of Garrick*

FROM THE EARLY YEARS OF THE EIGHTEENTH CENTURY ONWARD the theatres began to attract a much larger audience than they had done in Restoration days. Not only did the population of Britain increase from six millions in 1650 to ten millions in 1800, but the rise of the middle class enforced certain changes in the nature of theatrical entertainment. The loose morals and behaviour of Restoration Court circles gave way to more polite and respectable standards under Queen Anne, the result of which was that Court interest and influence in the theatre waned, and, subsequently, that the growing middle class, which formerly had stayed away, now began to patronize the theatres. Whatever may be said of Court circles in the days of Charles II, they certainly appreciated wit and poetry, and they generally had good taste in art. The same could not be said of the stolid, unimaginative middle class, and so the comedy of manners gave way to productions with more spectacular and sentimental qualities. The increase in the theatre-going public meant, of course, the building of new theatres, and the enlarging of those existing. During the century many new theatres were built in London and in all the larger towns of England. The fashionable resorts of Bath, Tunbridge Wells, and Brighton also had their theatres, and the provinces generally saw much thriving theatrical activity. The small select group of the community which formed the audience in Restoration days demanded a constant change of

F

bill and a continual flow of new plays. In Betterton's day plays were usually put on for one or two nights, very rarely running for a week, while in the eighteenth century the larger public created a longer run for the plays, and forty and fifty performances were not uncommon.

Although there was a change in the kind of play necessary to meet the demands of the new type of audiences, the actual mounting and presentation of the plays showed little radical alteration. The design and structure of the playhouses were not altered to any great extent, and the theatre in general underwent a pause in its development. It was a period of expansion rather than of change, and many of the old traditions of the Elizabethan stage were continued throughout the century.

Much of our knowledge of the theatre in the first half of the century is derived from Cibber's famous *Apology for the Life of Colley Cibber*. Cibber began acting in 1690 with Betterton, and eventually became the most popular personality in the theatre during the first three decades of the eighteenth century. Cibber had not the qualities of a great actor, but he was a good comedian, he could write successful comedies, and he was an excellent manager. In 1714, with Sir Richard Steele and three other actors, Wilks, Doggett, and Booth, he took over the management of the Theatre Royal, Drury Lane, of which he had already for some time been virtual manager. The theatre was still operating under the original royal patent, while the other patent operated at the old Lincoln's Inn Theatre, which seceding actors from Betterton's company had taken over in 1695. Among the shareholders of this company was Christopher Rich, a lawyer, who found the theatre a better business proposition than his law practice. Control of the Lincoln's Inn Theatre eventually passed to his son, John Rich.

Christopher Rich rebuilt the theatre, but it was not completed until shortly after his death in 1714; and his son appeared for the first time in a prologue at the opening of the new theatre, which gave as its first play Farquhar's *The Recruiting Officer*. The following year he made his only appearance as a tragedian, but it is his development of pantomime to which his fame is due. The new theatre began a successful policy of putting on an entirely new form of entertainment, composed of music, spectacle, dancing, and mime. It was, of course, not new in its elements, as Davenant in his so-called 'operas' had had similar ideas in mind; the form it took was an innovation. Rich took some of the characters from the *commedia dell' arte*, adapted them to conform with English conventions, and used them in comic scenes which were interwoven with rather dull allegorical plays, based on the lives and loves of various gods and goddesses. At first dialogue was used in the allegorical scenes of the production, but gradually music was introduced and recitative and arias found most suitable. The comic part of the operas, which was quite divorced from the rest, was entirely in dumb show, being devoted to the adventures of Harlequin and Columbine, Clown and Pantaloon. Rich himself was Harlequin, and he became famous for his dancing and miming in that rôle.

It was said that Rich developed his powers of miming because he had no voice, or that his voice was rough and uncultured, but, whatever the reason, his actions and gestures were so expressive that he did not need to speak. All writers of that period agree about his extraordinary powers of miming. Rich also made great strides in the staging of his productions, and used transformation scenes with surprising effect. At the touch of Harlequin's magic bat huts and cottages would be transformed into palaces, and temples and some of the characters changed into animals or articles of furniture, while gods and goddesses were continually descending to earth or being whisked up to the heavens. All of this was accomplished by the ingenious use of the flies and various trap-doors. Sound-effects played a great part, and there was much thunder, rainstorms, and roaring of seas, together with fire and lightning, not to mention the gentle fall of paper snow.

It is understandable that all this went down very well with the large, unsophisticated audiences of those days, and Rich had many years of complete success. His success was a constant source of worry to Drury Lane, and Cibber had to put on something similar. As far back as 1702 Drury Lane had presented an entertainment of dancing and action only, accompanied by music. The production was called *The Cheats of Scapin or the Tavern Bilkers*, and was created by John Weaver, a Shrewsbury dancing-master. Although at the time it was considered something of a novelty, the success of Rich's policy at Lincoln's Inn demanded more of Weaver's creations. In 1717 he presented ballets, as we would call them to-day, on the themes of Mars and Venus, Orpheus and Eurydice, and, a little later, Cupid and Bacchus. These productions were in addition to the plays presented in the same programme, and Cibber and his co-managers felt the need to apologize for them, which, as he said, " we generally use as crutches to our weakest plays." Apart from Rich's success as the English Harlequin (under the stage-name of Lun, the name of a noted French comedian), he was an enterprising manager, and was responsible in 1728 for the first production of John Gay's *The Beggar's Opera*, which ran at the Lincoln's Inn Theatre with great success for sixty-three nights. Cibber was mortified at this, as he had been offered the " Newgate pastoral," as it was called by Swift, and had declined to produce it. The receipts from the run of *The Beggar's Opera* were over £11,000, and with the spread of the news theatre managers were putting it on throughout the provinces, achieving runs of forty and fifty nights. Rich now began to look about for another house, and plans were made to build a new theatre, which would house a much larger audience, the site chosen being in the Covent Garden.

Rich raised the money required to build the new theatre by public subscription. The fifty subscribers made three payments of £100, and in return were to receive a rent of two shillings for every performance and, in addition, free seats anywhere in the house except behind the scenes. When one remembers that in Restoration days the public were permitted, on payment of a fee, to go behind the scenes to see the actors, one realizes that this was an important step, when even shareholders were confined to the front of the house. The new theatre was built, and opened in 1732 with a well-tried play, Congreve's *Way of the World*. It was the auditorium which had been enlarged in the new theatre; the stage remained the same, being actually made smaller, if anything, by the placing of seats on the apron. With the emphasis on spectacle and dumb show the actors would tend to retire behind the proscenium, their actions and movements being viewed immediately in front of the scenery. In contrast with Betterton's day, when the actors performed largely on the apron and the scenery was well in the background, they now became part of the stage picture. Also the seats on the apron stage, while still further evidence of the need to house more people, brought in half a guinea per seat, more than twice as much as the box seats. The pit remained at half a crown, and there were two galleries at two shillings and one shilling. In those days seats were not numbered or reserved, and a notice concerning the seats on the apron stage ran: " Servants will be allowed to keep places on the stage, and the ladies are desired to send them by 3 o'clock." As the performance began at 6 P.M. this seems to indicate that stage seats were very popular, at least with some section of the audience. When the doors of the theatre were thrown open there would be a concerted rush by the waiting crowd, and an excited scramble for the best seats would take place. The seats were backless benches, and since there was no central gangway a wild hurdle-race would ensue, in which the ladies, with their large hooped skirts, would be at a distinct disadvantage. The ladies would frequently lose their hats, and sometimes their shoes, in the struggle, and, once seated, quite a time would be spent in collecting and rearranging themselves. The competitive spirit so instilled into the audience put them on their mettle, and the play had to start with a bang or the players were soon greeted with a very noisy reception. The audiences were very lively and knew what they wanted—action and spectacle rather than wit and poetry.

Although the new house proved a success from the beginning, Rich kept on the Lincoln's Inn Theatre, but transferred the patent to Covent Garden. Drury Lane and Covent Garden were now the 'legitimate' theatres, with the monopoly of the spoken word. While the other theatres in town were legally allowed to present only pantomime, spectacle, and musical shows, there was at this time no hard-and-fast application of the rule, particularly as even the Drury Lane Theatre was forced to present pantomime instead of Shakespeare. Of the other theatres, the Haymarket, where Fielding's company played, had acquired a reputation for burlesques, opera, and musical shows. Fielding wrote some brilliantly satirical pieces for the stage, the best-known being *Tom Thumb the Great*, which ridiculed the kind of tragedy which was being continually played at the time, in which all the characters were killed off in the last scene. As long as he confined his satire to the contemporary stage, Fielding was safe, but when he turned to politics he was on very dangerous ground. It is said that Walpole passed the Licensing Act of 1737, which gave the Lord Chamberlain powers of censorship of all plays performed within the city of Westminster, because of the content of one of Fielding's plays. Anyhow, Fielding soon gave up writing for the stage and devoted his whole time to novel-writing.

It was at the Haymarket, which was open only during the summer months, when the other theatres were closed, that Handel had his seasons of opera. In addition to writing his own operas, Handel produced Italian operas, and scoured the Continent for singers. These seasons proved financially unsuccessful, and Handel got heavily into debt. On certain nights Rich leased the Covent Garden Theatre to Handel for the presentation of opera, and eventually he had a regular Lenten season for his sacred oratorios. It was here, in 1743, that the *Messiah* had its first London performance. These seasons proved very successful, and became an institution; Handel was able to recuperate his past losses, to pay all his debts, and to retire with a comfortable income. After his death the oratorios were continued, and ever since Covent Garden has been linked with the names of some of the greatest singers of the times.

The year 1740 saw the debut at Covent Garden of the celebrated Peg Woffington. She had appeared in London before, at the Haymarket, when at the age of fifteen she performed as a member of the juvenile troupe of the famous Madame Violante. After years of touring the country she eventually settled down in the theatre at Dublin, where she achieved great fame, especially in the part of Sir Harry Wildair in Farquhar's *Constant Couple*. On coming to London she called at Rich's house nineteen times, without giving her name, and each time she was refused an interview. When Rich finally knew who his persistent caller really was he, being an astute manager, invited her in and acquired her services for the Covent Garden at the modest salary of nine pounds per week. Rich was rather an eccentric in private life, and Peg, recording her visit, describes him lounging on a sofa with a cup of tea in one hand, from which he took occasional sips, and a book in the other; he was surrounded by no fewer than twenty-seven cats, which walked all over the sofa, climbed on to his lap and his shoulders, and even sipped his tea. Peg's debut was in the rôle of Sylvia in *The Recruiting Officer*, a part in which she appears for several scenes in male costume. As this suited her sparkling and vivacious personality, following on her success in Dublin as Sir Harry Wildair, she began to play men's rôles in other plays. From then onward the 'breeches' part was an accepted convention, and most leading actresses were prepared to assume occasionally a male rôle.

Some years previously another famous actress began her career at Drury Lane. Mrs Cibber was a sister of the composer Thomas Arne and the wife of Colley Cibber's son Theophilus. She was trained by her father-in-law and played in both comedy and tragedy, while she had such a fine voice that it is said that Handel specially arranged the contralto songs in the *Messiah* for her. Between the two patent theatres there was a good deal of co-operation at this time, and by mutual arrangement actors played at both theatres. In 1742 Rich acquired Mrs Cibber's services, and she played in tragedies with Quin, who was then Rich's leading tragic actor.

In the previous year there happened an event in the theatrical world which shook the management of both theatres; a new star had arisen at the Goodman's Fields Theatre, the advent of whom caused such a sensation that the receipts of both Drury Lane and Covent Garden showed an immediate and precipitate decline. David Garrick had arrived. At the age of twenty-four he was playing Richard III, being billed as " a gentleman who never appeared on any stage."

This was not strictly true, as for several years he had gained experience in amateur theatricals, and had played under an assumed name in provincial theatres. Half French and half Irish by descent, Garrick was the son of an army captain, and had received a good education (he and his brother had been the first pupils at the private school set up by Dr Johnson); he was in appearance rather short, but extremely handsome. His business sense was very apparent in his acquiring the foundations of his art in the provinces under an assumed name; and in making his debut in London he took the town by storm. The secret was, of course, that he had developed an entirely fresh approach to acting. The playgoing public, now a little tired with so much spectacle and with the rather heavy, stilted style of such leading actors as Wilks, Booth, and Quin, found something quite new in Garrick's approach. The Goodman's Fields Theatre played to such crowded houses that the two patent theatres had to do something quickly in order to stop the fall in their receipts. After going through the necessary legal formalities they successfully invoked their monopoly rights, with the result that Giffard, the manager of Goodman's Fields, had to cut the season short and close the theatre, whereupon Fleetwood, the wealthy, irresponsible youth who was now managing Drury Lane, persuaded Garrick to join his company, at the colossal salary (for those days)

QUIN AS CORIOLANUS

of six hundred guineas a season. Garrick seized his opportunity and set forth on a series of rôles in Shakespearean and contemporary plays, which he interpreted in an entirely fresh manner, although not without some opposition from Macklin, who had until then been the leading actor in the company, and whose acting belonged to the old traditional style. Macklin, however, was later to come under the influence of Garrick and to revolutionize the portrayal of Shylock by giving him tragic qualities. Peg Woffington, after having quarrelled with Rich, had left Covent Garden and had also joined the Drury Lane company, and an attachment was formed with Garrick which eventually blossomed into a love affair. It did not culminate in marriage, unfortunately for Peg, but it possibly had an effect on Garrick's move to Dublin two years later. Fleetwood, ever a bad manager, had got into arrears with the players' salaries, and although Garrick had led the company on strike, matters were not settled satisfactorily.

In 1745 Garrick left the Drury Lane Theatre and accepted an offer of another season in Dublin. Here he was enthusiastically received by Irish audiences and added further to his laurels. In June of the following year he returned to London for a short season with Rich at the Covent Garden. For only six perform-ances, five of which were Shakespearean rôles—King Lear, Hamlet, Richard III, Othello, and Macbeth—Garrick and Rich each netted £300. After a period of management chiefly devoted to pantomime and spectacle drama was back with a vengeance. The following season Garrick was naturally re-engaged, and played alternately with Quin. Mrs Cibber was also in the company, and with her Garrick began a long and happy partnership. On October 20 Quin played Richard III, and on October 31 Garrick played the same part, giving the public the chance to compare the two greatly differing styles. One cannot but admire the showmanship of Rich in thus presenting the new and the old in the theatre. Here is a contem-porary description of Quin:

MACKLIN AS SHYLOCK

> Quin presented himself upon the rising of the curtain in a green velvet coat, embroidered down the seams, an enormous full-bottom periwig, rolled stockings, and high-heeled, square-toed shoes; with very little variation of cadence, and in deep, full tones, accompanied by a sawing kind of motion which had more of the senate than the stage in it, he rolled out his heroics with an air of dignified indifference that seemed to disdain the plaudits bestowed upon him.

And of Garrick:

> When, after long and eager expectation, I first beheld little Garrick, then young and light, and alive in every muscle and in every feature, come bounding on the stage . . . Heavens, what a transition! It seemed as if a whole century had been stepped over in the changing of a single scene—old things were done away, and a new order at once brought forward, light and luminous, and clearly destined to dispel the barbarisms and bigotry of a tasteless age, too long . . . superstitiously devoted to the illusions of imposing declamation.

Garrick had broken all the rules, upset stage convention, and by his naturalistic acting had won over the public. Quin, although he was a good enough actor in his own style, suffered the humiliation of seeing receipts on Garrick's nights increase with every performance, while on the nights he played they fell in equivalent proportion. It says a lot for Quin's good-nature that he and Garrick got on quite well together, and that throughout the entire season there was no sign of enmity between them. At the end of the season Garrick bought a share in the patent of the Drury Lane Theatre, and in 1747 he assumed management.

Garrick had persuaded Mrs Cibber to join the Drury Lane company, which also included

DAVID GARRICK

Peg Woffington, lively Kitty Clive, of whom Dr Johnson said, " She was a better romp than any I ever saw in nature," Mrs Pritchard, Delane, Yates, and Macklin. At thirty Garrick was leading actor and manager of the most brilliant company of players in the theatre of the time. He ruled the company with an iron hand, and by careful training of the players in his own ways of acting, and by the force of his overriding personality, he achieved a unity in the production of plays which has rarely been exceeded in the history of the theatre. He continued his repertoire of Shakespearean rôles with great success, and he also found time to write over forty plays of his own, few of which proved failures when produced. After many years of public acclaim Garrick suddenly tired of London and set off on a grand tour of France and Italy. This lasted two years, in which he played with his company in most of the principal cities, with continual welcome and success.

In 1765 he returned from his triumphs abroad to Drury Lane, bringing with him a mass of new ideas for revolutionizing the stage. England had always been behind the European theatres with her stage technique, and just as Inigo Jones and Davenant found new ideas in the theatres of France and Italy, so Garrick returned ready to equip the Drury Lane stage with the latest Continental innovations.

There had already been some development since the Restoration stage, chiefly because of

GARRICK AND MRS CIBBER IN "VENICE PRESERVED"

the need to house more of the public. The apron stage, with its two doors on either side of the proscenium, was diminished to half its former depth, and the two doors were reduced to one. The tendency was for the actors to play more and more behind the proscenium and to be seen against the scenery. The scenery itself had by now progressed from Davenant's simple and easily movable flats or shutters, and solid doors and windows were now constructed in the flats. Garrick realized that the tendency of the actors mentioned above put them farther away from the audience, so that the finer points of acting were lost, and by his lighting innovations he somewhat counteracted the tendency. First of all he removed the great hoops of candles, which provided illumination to auditorium and stage alike, and hung them behind the proscenium arch out of sight of the audience. The main result of concealing the chief source of lighting, which hitherto had always been a cause of irritation to the folk in the gallery, was to make the stage easier to see, while incidentally heightening the dramatic effect. He also placed lights behind the wings, on a level with the actors, and likewise concealed from the audience. Other innovations were the greater use of oil-lamps, and coloured transparent silks for producing coloured lighting effects. Garrick also made greater use of the footlights, for although they had been introduced in England many years before, their use was not universal, and even in the new Covent Garden Theatre of 1732 they were not installed. A further introduction was the use of lanterns and wall-brackets as an integral part of the setting, which also provided more light on the stage. Briefly, the effect of Garrick's innovations was more light on the actors and less on the audience. Garrick made many other innovations on the stage itself, which were all intended to further naturalistic representation.

Up to the middle of the eighteenth century scenery had been quite conventional. Wherever the scene of the play took place, in foreign countries, in palace or chamber, in market-place or in humble cottage, the scenic artist painted conventional architectural settings, with no regard for either style or period. Garrick's influence on stage design was manifest when his scenic artist De Loutherbourg took a sketching trip to Derbyshire in order to provide material for what were then regarded as highly realistic settings. Another designer of that time, Capon, produced settings to which some thought had been given regarding historical accuracy. He produced designs in which houses were painted as they might have appeared in the past, and he paid particular attention to the Gothic style of architecture. Here were the first tentative beginnings of the great quest for realism on the stage which was ultimately reached at the end of the following century.

Strangely enough, there was little development in stage costume throughout the century. Garrick played all his great Shakespearean rôles in the elaborate costume of his own day. Costumes of an earlier period were never worn even when called for by the action of the play. This may have been due to the demands of the audience, for when in 1773 Macklin appeared at Covent Garden as Macbeth, clad in correct Scottish costume, he was greeted with boos, hisses, and a storm of disapproval. Some progress was made in women's costume, which up to 1734 had been strictly à la mode. For a long time no actress would dare to wear anything but the very latest fashion, whatever the period of the play. In 1734 a ballet dancer, Mlle Sallé, at Covent Garden, discarded the enormous hooped skirt and the fashionable piled-up coiffure of false hair. She wore her own hair, unpowdered, simply arranged, and without ornament, while she was dressed in a bodice and petticoat, over which a simple robe of muslin was carefully draped after the model of a Greek statue. While this freedom was dictated by the needs of dancing, it also met with approval from the audience. The lighter forms of entertainment, pantomime and ballet, had their special costumes, which were conventional rather than historical, but in tragedy the costume was the current vogue. It was left to Mrs Siddons, towards the end of the century, to introduce more freedom and variety into women's dress on the stage.

Soon after his return from the Continent Garrick retired from acting, but remained a very active manager at Drury Lane. The public, however, clamoured for his return to the stage, and six months later George III issued a royal command to Garrick to resume acting, which he could not ignore. He continued acting until he finally left the stage in 1776. Garrick amassed a considerable fortune, and built a large house at Hampton, which still stands, together with the delightful little temple he erected in the grounds, on the river-bank, as a tribute to Shakespeare, to whom he owed so much of his success. Garrick did much to raise the social status of players, who now began to regard themselves no longer as servants of the aristocracy, but more as equals. The institution of the green room, the salon in which the players could meet interested members of the upper classes during the intervals of their appearance on the stage, had its origin in Restoration days, in the scene-room described by Pepys. It is not known why this particular colour was chosen for the room, but during the eighteenth century green was a very popular colour in the theatre. Tragedies were always played on a green carpet, the stage curtain itself was green, and the stage attendants, who moved the furniture and changed the scenery, also wore green livery.

GARRICK AS MACBETH

It is due chiefly to Garrick that the theatre banished those snobs of high society from their privileged seats on the stage, which since Shakespeare's day had caused embarrassment to the actors and ill-feeling in the pit. The only persons, apart from the actors, who could be seen on the stage after this reform were the green-liveried stage attendants and the guards who in days of riot in the theatre stood at both sides of the stage, as a first line of defence from the pit. There is a story that one of these guardsmen was so overcome by the strength of Garrick's acting in a certain tragedy that he fell in a faint. Garrick afterwards sent for the man and, sympathizing with his embarrassment, presented him with a guinea. The news soon got around, and the following night another guardsman collapsed. Unfortunately for him, he had not realized that this night Garrick was playing in a comedy, and so the guinea was not forthcoming. Guardsmen were also used to keep order outside the doors of the theatre, for in those days, of course, there was no police force to carry out these duties. To-day guardsmen are still employed by the theatres, not as custodians of the peace, but as supers in large productions such as operas, when numbers of soldiers are required on the stage. Even in early Victorian times, on the occasion of a royal visit to the theatre, a Yeoman of the Guard would stand at either side of the stage during the performance.

The first seventy years of the eighteenth century produced few plays of lasting value. Writers had discovered the novel and essay as a new form for their endeavours, and while such writers as Pope and Johnson wrote plays, they were too literary in quality to live as drama. The Augustan period, as it was called, produced the grand and heroic figures that actors such as Booth, Wilks, and Quin interpreted by heavy, stilted acting. The fresh, romantic approach of Garrick had little counterpart in the writings of the opposing school, as exemplified in poetry by Shelley. The best writers generally neglected the theatre, and the whole century produced only three comedies which have acquired universal acclaim— Goldsmith's *She Stoops to Conquer* and Sheridan's *The Rivals* and *The School for Scandal*.

Goldsmith's play was first produced at Covent Garden in 1773. The manager, Colman, had accepted the play with misgivings, owing to the very moderate success of Goldsmith's earlier play, *The Good Natur'd Man*, and had delayed presenting it for over a year. Owing to Dr Johnson's persistent and enthusiastic influence, Colman at last put the play into rehearsal, and, while still seeing no merit in the play, presented it on March 15, 1773. It was an immediate success, and the Press and public were full of acclaim. Besides being a good play, it had the humorous and rather sentimental qualities of the happy ending, which were much appreciated by the large popular audiences. Poor Goldsmith was unable to enjoy his first real financial success for long, as the following year he died, at the age of forty-six.

Richard Brinsley Sheridan was born in 1751, the son of Thomas Sheridan, an actor of the old school, who had played at both Covent Garden and Drury Lane, where for a time he was stage-manager under Garrick. In 1773 Sheridan married a singer, Elizabeth Linley, who had sung in oratorios at Covent Garden. Her father, Dr Linley, was a distinguished musician, and his talent was passed on to his children. *The Rivals* was produced at Covent Garden for the first time in 1775, and although the first night was not a success, when alterations had been made in the cast and the dialogue speeded up it immediately rose in public favour. The following year Garrick retired from Drury Lane, and Sheridan managed to raise the money to buy his share of the patent. He moved in with his whole family, his wife as accounts-keeper, his father-in-law as musical director, and Mrs Linley as wardrobe mistress. His father, old Thomas Sheridan, was installed as stage-manager, while his own position was that of supervisor and playwright. The first season at Drury Lane saw the production of his masterpiece, *The School for Scandal*, which brought Sheridan a large amount of money and an international reputation as a playwright. The same year he wrote *The Duenna*, an opera, with music by Dr Linley, which was produced at Covent Garden. *The Critic*, a comedy based largely on the Duke of Buckingham's farce, *The Rehearsal*, soon followed. As this play burlesques the stage of the earlier days, and in particular the rhyming tragedies of Dryden, it is rarely revived now. *Pizarro*, his only tragedy, is also rarely revived, as it has few lasting qualities, although at the time it was written it achieved popularity.

Sheridan gave up writing for the stage at the age of twenty-eight, and henceforth confined his activities to management. His sparkling wit and social qualities were not to be lost to the nation, however, for in 1780 he entered Parliament, and distinguished himself as an orator and a master of debate, notably at the impeachment of Warren Hastings. His interest in the theatre declined, and he became a thoroughly bad manager. He dressed and lived in a style totally beyond his means, and played an active part in the theatre only when receipts began to fall and his way of living was in danger. Thus in 1791 he rebuilt the theatre,

"THE SCHOOL FOR SCANDAL" ON THE DRURY LANE STAGE 1777

THE AUDITORIUM OF DRURY LANE AT THE SAME PERIOD

making room for 3600 people, instead of 2000 as previously, and the stage had a pro-scenium opening of forty-three feet. In spite of numerous fire precautions, water-taps well distributed throughout, and an iron curtain, in 1809 the theatre caught fire and burned to the ground. At the time Sheridan first heard the news he was debating in Parliament on

the war in Spain, and it is typical of the man that he stayed on until the House adjourned, returning to find the theatre a smouldering shell. Sheridan was now completely ruined, and he remained bankrupt until his death in 1816—a rather depress-ing end to a brilliant beginning. In 1812 a new theatre was built on the site by Samuel Whitbread, the brewer, and although considerably altered, it remains there to-day.

During Garrick's last years at Drury Lane he was continually on the look-out for fresh talent. Owing to his ill-health and declining years, the leading actresses of the company were getting a little out of hand, so he decided to introduce into the theatre a young and beautiful actress who had been playing in the provinces. He had first heard of Mrs Siddons when she was playing at a small theatre at Cheltenham. He followed her travels about the country and sent out agents to report her progress for a whole year before deciding to

MRS SIDDONS

offer her an engagement. Mrs Siddons, at the age of twenty and already a mother, made her debut at Drury Lane in December 1775, as Portia, in *The Merchant of Venice*. Although young, she was not without experience; born of a theatrical family, the Roger Kembles, who had quite a provincial reputation, she had first appeared on the stage at a very early age. All through her childhood acting with her parents alternated with periods when she was sent away to school. This training gave her an easy facility for remembering lines, a clear and pleasing voice, and a passion for Milton and the classic poets. Her parents naturally encouraged and developed her talents for the stage, and were not a little disappointed when, at the age of eighteen, she married a rather second-rate actor, William Siddons. The young couple left the Kembles and joined another company touring the West of England. It was with this company that Mrs Siddons was discovered at Cheltenham in the sum-mer of 1774.

When she at last arrived at Drury Lane Garrick was pleased with her appearance, paid her compliments, and recognized both her promise and her inexperience of large theatres. Although he gave her every encouragement, her debut was doomed to failure. Poor Sarah was in a panic and was a bundle of nerves. She walked on to the stage, a tall, slender, and rather gawky figure, and immediately her voice began to fail. Her lines died off in a whisper, and, in addition, she became so nervous that she completely forgot her actions and movements. The play dragged on and came to a depressing end. Except for one newspaper, the Press confirmed the public reaction to a disappointing first appearance, the solitary exception being written by a friend of Garrick's who had seen her in the provinces. In spite of the bad beginning, Garrick decided to continue her engagement all through the season, and in one of his own farewell performances, towards the end of the season, she played opposite him. Garrick spent a considerable time giving her instructions, and on her spare evenings she would watch his acting from the special box with which he had provided her. Her misfortune, however, continued throughout the season, and she had no better reception from Press or public. And when Sheridan took over management at the end of the season her services were not retained.

EIGHTEENTH-CENTURY COSTUME FOR "THE COUNTRY WIFE"

With a heavy heart she set off again with her husband for the provinces, determined at least to make a success in the flourishing theatres of Birmingham, York, Liverpool, and the other large towns. After periods of local success, illness, and confinement, she finally settled down at Bath, which was then becoming a centre of fashion, elegance, and scandal. Her success among this critical public was immediate. She worked hard, and gave creditable performances in Shakespearean parts and in contemporary plays. She played for four seasons at Bath, and during this time her art was slowly maturing. Her intellectual powers developed gradually, and, with increasing experience and the time to develop her own approach to acting, she acquired a new sense of confidence with the knowledge of her own powers of restraint. In 1780 Thomas Sheridan came to Bath for his health, and on seeing Mrs Siddons act was so struck with her development that he hastened back to persuade his son to engage her for Drury Lane. Sarah was a success at Bath and had many friends in the town, so she was not easily persuaded to give up the certainty of a small but regular income for an uncertainty in London. No doubt, too, she had thoughts of her previous disappointment. Finally, two years later, she agreed to accept an engagement from Sheridan, and said farewell to her enthusiastic audiences in Bath, who were greatly disappointed at her leaving. At her farewell performance she produced on the stage her three "reasons" for accepting the London engagement—her three small children.

Her first reappearance at Drury Lane was in the leading part of Isabella in the play of that name, a version by Garrick of Southerne's *Fatal Marriage*, in which grief and tears were predominant. On the evening of the first night her father, Roger Kemble, turned up to comfort her and to allay her fears and worries. Although she was inwardly quaking with thoughts of her past experience at the enormous theatre, she walked on to the stage and began

to immerse herself completely into the part. It was a part that gave her magnificent oppor-
tunities for displaying her pathos and tragic qualities, and with her now well-matured style
she gave a great performance. The audience was deeply moved, and before the curtain
descended spontaneous applause broke out all over the theatre. Sarah Siddons had returned
to triumph.

MRS SIDDONS AS ELVIRA IN "PIZARRO"

The Press followed public opinion and was full of enthusiastic notices, Sarah being placed
even above the great Mrs Cibber. Her success at Drury Lane now complete and her future
assured, she remained playing leading parts for the next twenty years. At twenty-seven
Mrs Siddons was tall and slender, though not angular in figure, with graceful movements,
while her head was small, with classic features and dark, compelling eyes. At the close of
her first season she went to Dublin, accepting a summer engagement at the Smock Alley
Theatre, where she was to meet her eldest brother, John Philip Kemble. Kemble had com-

pleted his education in France and then set out to conquer the stage. His first important engagement was in Dublin, and on the strength of his successful seasons there Sheridan booked him for Drury Lane. In the autumn they both returned to London and began a long period of successes. Like his sister, Kemble was tall, handsome, and dignified in appearance, and his style of acting was in a way a reversion from Garrick's easy, naturalistic flexibility to the more classic style of the earlier actors. Both Sarah and John found their greatest successes in tragic rôles, particularly in Shakespearean plays, and until the early nineteenth century they remained the undisputed leaders of the stage in this country.

Mrs Siddons made several innovations in women's costume in the theatre. She was the first woman to discard the powdered hair and large hooped skirts of the time. She developed costumes of a simple shape, based on classic models, and designed simply draped head-dresses to replace the elaborate, beplumed helmets which were traditional wear with the tragic actresses of the past. Her costumes were in no sense historically accurate, but they were no longer of the latest fashion, and were specially designed for acting and the stage.

During the century the use of the large apron stage declined and scenery became more realistic, taking up more space on the stage. Acting began to lose the freedom of movement possible on the Restoration stage, and the concentration of light on the actors, well behind the proscenium, also tended to confine acting space. Many more theatres were built for a growing middle-class public, whose taste unfortunately discouraged great drama, so that few plays of lasting value were written. The demands of the audiences made necessary a long bill, which often included a full five-act tragedy, a comic piece, and a ballet or pantomime, together with interludes of dancing or music and the various prologues and epilogues. The audiences were lively and vociferous, and if they took a dislike to anything or anybody, instead of just staying away from the theatre they would pay for admission night after night in order to create a disturbance or start a riot, in which they would try to invade the stage and stop the performances. Indeed, riots were common in the theatres throughout the century. At a trial of the ring-leaders of a riot at the Haymarket in 1738 the law declared " that the public had a legal right to manifest their dislike to any play or actor; and that the judicature of the pit had been acquiesced in, time immemorial." The public were very conscious of their rights, and actors and managers were compelled to bow to their demands. The occasional invasions of the stage by unruly members of the pit made necessary the provision of spiked railings over the orchestra, and such decorative ironware as that on the front of the Drury Lane stage served to hinder their destructive efforts. One of the most serious disturbances occurred in 1755, when a company of French dancers was being presented by Garrick at the Drury Lane Theatre. At this time England was drifting into war with France, and the audience in pit and galleries showed their disapproval by six nights of prolonged rioting. Garrick appealed to the better instincts of the gathering, and received support from the fashionable folk in the boxes. This incensed the pit and galleries, and fighting broke out among the two factions. Gallants jumped into the pit from the boxes, swords were drawn, and blood was shed, when suddenly all were united in a common purpose to do as much damage as possible. Benches were torn up and scenery demolished, the damage amounting to several thousand pounds.

G

Even in normal times the audience was hardly well behaved. It was a common practice for the galleries to pelt unpopular people in the pit with orange-peel or rotten fruit. Quarrels were frequent among people in different parts of the theatre, while there was a continual calling-out and impatient knocking of sticks on the floor until the curtain rose. It follows that under these conditions the actors, whatever their style, had to be good; and it was to acting that the century made its greatest contribution.

# CHAPTER SEVEN

## The Victorians

## CHAPTER SEVEN
# THE VICTORIANS

IN THE SUMMER OF 1802, unable to stand any longer the continual wrangles with Sheridan over payment of their salaries, Kemble and Mrs Siddons left Drury Lane for good. Kemble managed to raise sufficient money to purchase a sixth share in the Covent Garden patent, which brought with it the chance not only of acting, but, as stage-manager, of deciding who should play with him. While negotiations were being completed Kemble made a holiday tour of the Continent and Sarah went to Ireland. They both returned to London to commence the 1803 season, Kemble first appearing in *Hamlet* with great success, followed soon after by Mrs Siddons as Isabella in *The Fatal Marriage*. As a manager Kemble was tactful and considerate, in spite of the excesses of George Frederick Cooke, an actor with a reputation second only to Kemble's. Cooke had an uncontrollable temper and drank heavily, but when sober and in suitable parts he gave extremely good performances. His passionate and erratic acting was a marked contrast to the studied calm and dignity of Kemble's style. The first season went well; among the list of plays produced, eleven were by Shakespeare, an indication that public taste was for drama rather than spectacle. Soon the pendulum was to swing back, but for the moment acting was the all-important element in the theatre.

The following season both Mrs Siddons and Kemble were eclipsed by a brighter, though much smaller, star. An infant prodigy known as Master Betty, or " the Young Roscius," had sprung into public notice in the provinces, where he had been appearing with great success. Although only about thirteen years of age, he was playing leading parts with grown actors, and his fame had swept the country. He had come from Belfast, where a year or two earlier he had seen Mrs Siddons play and had been so struck with her acting that he decided to take up the stage himself. Kemble engaged him for Covent Garden, where his success with the public was so great that Kemble presented him in all his own great tragic

GRIMALDI IN "MOTHER GOOSE"

rôles. Betty seems to have had a keen business-man for a father, for when he appeared at Covent Garden he received fifty guineas a night. On alternate nights he also played at Drury Lane, where he commanded an even greater salary. London went completely mad about Betty, and the climax came when Pitt adjourned the House of Commons, which then went in a body to see Betty play Hamlet. Betty is said to have been able to portray changing emotions well, and his action was good, but his face showed little or no expression and his lines were delivered in a sing-song fashion, a style which had been popular early in the eighteenth century. It was probably the novelty of seeing a tiny, slender figure in place of the usual stalwart tragedian rather than Betty's qualities as an actor, clever little boy though he must have been, which attracted the audience. His success lasted until the end of the following season, when the public grew tired of the little hero, and although he played a year or two longer in the provinces he soon vanished quietly from the scene.

A year or so later Covent Garden produced its most successful pantomime, *Mother Goose*, in which Joe Grimaldi established his reputation as the greatest low comedian of the day. Grimaldi's father had been employed by Garrick at Drury Lane, and young Joe, being brought up in the theatre, was already a highly accomplished and experienced actor by the time he was in his middle twenties. He had played at Drury Lane and Sadler's Wells and minor theatres, chiefly in pantomime. In *Mother Goose* the principal character was not, as in the pantomime of Rich's day, Harlequin, but Clown, and Grimaldi portrayed this character with all the skill of by-play, dumb show, and subtle gesticulation. He was responsible for the curious costume and make-up which has been adapted and imitated by all subsequent clowns, nowadays only to be seen at the circus or variety show. Grimaldi's subtlety of action and movement was such that even Kemble took private lessons from him, as did certain gentlemen of the Court.

*Mother Goose* was only part of the evening's programme, being usually preceded by a full-length tragedy and a comic ballet. The popularity of the pantomime enabled it to run for ninety-two performances, during which period the accompanying pieces were changed many times. There thus began a tendency to spend much more money on scenery, costumes, and properties for pantomime than for tragedy, in which the personality and skill of the actor were held to be sufficient attraction. The long bill led to the practice of admitting the public at half-price midway through the evening's entertainment. Thus those members of the public who wished to see the pantomime only could do so at a lower charge and be encouraged to see it not merely once but several times.

In 1808 Kemble's subsequent misfortunes began when the firing of a gun on the stage set some scenery smouldering, which burst into flame early in the morning, the fire with great rapidity consuming the entire building. All the contents of the theatre were destroyed, including the valuable scenery, costumes, and properties, Kemble's extensive library of books and manuscripts, and a vast collection of music by Handel, Arne, and other musicians who had been associated with the theatre in the past. Gone too was Handel's great organ, that he had bequeathed to Rich after a long and happy collaboration. Mrs Siddons lost her entire collection of stage jewellery and costumes.

Evidence of public concern and esteem for the two great stars was soon forthcoming, however, and public subscriptions for the rebuilding of the theatre poured in. The company moved to the King's Theatre, in the Haymarket, while money was being raised for the new theatre. Insurance claims brought in about half of the necessary capital, and within a year the new theatre was actually completed. The new building was designed in the prevailing classic style of architecture, fronted by a huge Doric portico. The row of dwelling-houses that originally screened the theatre in Bow Street having also been burnt down, the extra space available was used to enlarge the interior, grand anterooms and salons being added for "the comfort and convenience" of the public. There were three tiers of boxes as well as the two galleries, and two central gangways made the pit more easily accessible. The third tier was made up of twenty-three 'private boxes,' each with its own anteroom and furnished with chairs, the latter a great innovation in those days, as hitherto the seating accommodation, even in the boxes, consisted of rows of backless benches. The house was illuminated with forty glass chandeliers, each holding many candles. Not only was the auditorium made much grander, but the stage was considerably enlarged, the proscenium opening being about forty feet wide, and the depth of the stage from the footlights to the back wall was increased to nearly seventy feet. The theatre, when full, held an audience of nearly three thousand, and the entire cost of rebuilding and furnishing amounted to over £300,000.

As less than half the money had been raised, the new theatre began its life under a heavy burden of debt, and this led to an increase in the prices of admission, which was to provoke a storm of public disapproval, and Kemble's subsequent eclipse in the favour of the public.

The theatre opened on September 18, 1809, with *Macbeth*, followed by a musical farce called *The Quaker*. No sooner had Kemble appeared on the stage to make the customary opening address than pandemonium broke out. To prove that it was a premeditated course of action, many members of the audience produced hand-bells, watchmen's rattles, and all

THE NEW COVENT GARDEN THEATRE IN 1810

kinds of noisy instruments. Placards were produced declaring their demand of " Old Prices "
or " Kemble, Tremble," and the audience kept up a continual chant of " O.P.," accompanied
by a regular beat of stamping feet or blows on the floor. Although the demonstration was
chiefly directed against Kemble and Mrs Siddons, with admirable self-control the company
went on with the performance of the play, although they were quite inaudible. This disturbance continued night after night, and Kemble, determined not to be beaten by the mob,
had Bow Street runners in the house to arrest the ringleaders. In spite of this the riots continued, and Kemble was forced to put on a programme entirely composed of dumb show.
Throughout the season the demonstrations continued, even the introduction of prize-fighters
hired by Kemble failing to put an end to them, though a temporary lull was effected by the
appearance of the darling of the public, Grimaldi. The Press was divided on the issue, taking
both sides, and many were the cartoons and prints published satirizing the whole affair.
Kemble submitted his books to an impartial committee of influential persons, including the
Solicitor-General and the Governor of the Bank of England, to prove how speculative theatre
management really was, and that he was justified in raising the prices of admission. The
committee published their report, completely confirming Kemble's action, but all to no
purpose, for the nightly cry of " O.P." continued.

Finally Kemble had to bow to public demand, and on meeting three hundred of the
rioters at a dinner at the Crown and Anchor Tavern he signed a paper agreeing to their

demands. The public apology that followed from the stage was greeted with a placard hoisted in the pit on which was written " We are satisfied."

The disturbances were not entirely due to the increase in prices, as the two galleries had remained at the old price. From the ranks of the pit the leaders of the riots gave vent to their disapproval, not only of the increased prices, but also of the innovation of ' private ' boxes, the employment of a foreign singer, and later, of course, of the strong-arm methods used to counter the rioters by means of pugilists. The galleries followed the lead of the pit, and they had an additional complaint in their poor view of the stage, due to the increased height of the galleries, which was necessitated by the extra tier of ' private ' boxes.

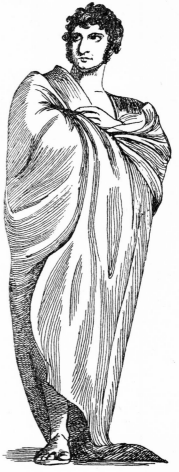

The ' private ' boxes were let for the season, and brought in about £10,000 a year. As Kemble was forced to abolish them, the loss of this considerable income had to be made up somehow, and inevitably he turned to what we to-day call the " box-office draw." The fact that pantomime, burlesque, and the lighter forms of entertainment were becoming increasingly popular, and that the minor theatres were booming, together with the success of Astley's Amphitheatre, where horses and other animals provided the entertainment, all supplied the reasons for Kemble's production of *Bluebeard* in 1811, complete with sixteen horses. The following year an elephant appeared on the stage in another pantomime at the theatre. Although this greatly appealed to the public the stage mechanic of Drury Lane, making a comment on the inevitable triumph of art over nature, said that he would be sorry if he could not design and construct a moving animal greatly superior in every degree.

In the same year Mrs Siddons retired from the stage, at the age of fifty-six. After over forty years of acting she had attained a unique position in the history of the theatre. In the ' grand manner,' which she had established with her brother,

KEMBLE AS CORIOLANUS

she remained unsurpassed, and she was the first notable actress to lead a blameless and normal life. Her final performance was as Lady Macbeth, and in accordance with the custom at that time the play came to an end immediately after her final exit in the sleepwalking scene, when the audience, as a compliment to the great actress, insisted on the performance coming to an end. Mrs Siddons reappeared, after changing her costume, to make a farewell speech, specially written for her in verse by her nephew, Horace Twiss. She retired with a comfortable income to enjoy her last years in peace and quiet. Even in retirement, however, the stage still attracted her, and she made occasional appearances, chiefly at benefit performances for other actors, appearing in the popular tragedy *Douglas* as late as 1819. She died in 1831.

Kemble never recaptured his popularity after the ' O.P.' riots, and although he continued acting, he was an ageing and disappointed man. He retired in 1817, receiving an ovation as great as his sister's, and died in 1823. Kemble as an actor had an appearance stately and picturesque, though possessing a rather husky voice, and represented on the stage the pseudo-classical interest that was so greatly influencing architecture and painting at the time. His deportment and pose were modelled on Roman sculpture rather than on Roman life. As a manager his reputation rests on his presentation of Shakespeare's plays. He tried to dress the players in costumes of varying periods, and he spent considerable care and time in making the settings appropriate. Garrick had played Shakespeare in modern costume and had spent more money on his pantomimes, preferring to rely on his acting alone to draw the crowds to Shakespeare. Garrick restored Shakespeare to his former importance in the theatre, and Kemble and Mrs Siddons continued to keep the great tragedies before the public.

In 1800 there were only ten theatres in London; by 1840 there were twenty-two. Although this was partly due to the increase in the population of London, then growing rapidly, it was also due to the theatre's increasing attraction for a rather different class of audience. We have seen how, in the early eighteenth century, the Court influence declined in the theatre, being succeeded by that of the upper middle class, until eventually this section of the community also lost interest in the theatre. By the early years of the nineteenth century polite society generally stayed away from the theatres, which now, much enlarged, housed great numbers of the working classes. As evidenced by Kemble's experience at Covent Garden, the audiences were emphatic in their likes and dislikes, and this had no little effect on drama at the time. The custom of 'giving out' after the play, although traditional and dating back to Restoration days, was in a way the managers' safeguard against the tyranny of the audience. At the close of the play a representative of the management, often the stage-manager, would announce the repetition of the performance on subsequent nights, and the nature of his reception from the very vociferous audience usually decided the fate of the production. Several great writers of the time, including Dickens and Browning, were to hear the hissing and booing that marked the reception of their plays, and, naturally, decided to confine their activities to the much safer practice of publication. On the other hand, there were plenty of hack writers in the theatre successfully writing melodramas, burlesques, and other forms of light entertainment. Much of the work was adapted from French comedies and farces, and there was a great deal of 'pirating' of plays written in this country. Until the Authors Act was passed by Parliament in 1832 there were no acting rights, and when an author presented a new play to a manager he received only an agreed sum. Authors had no claim on other managers who might send their servants to make a copy of the play from the performances at the theatre and later present it in a rather mangled form at their own theatres. There was no serious writing for the English stage for about the first forty years of the century, partly because of these reasons, but also because of theatrical monopoly.

Those ghosts of the Restoration theatre, the Killigrew and Davenant patents, still persisted, and the managers of Drury Lane and Covent Garden held the exclusive rights to present spoken drama. Apart from the Haymarket, which was open only in the summer, when the patent theatres were closed, all the other so-called minor theatres in London were obliged to present only 'illegitimate' drama, or entertainment in which any dialogue spoken had to be accompanied by music. The minor theatres were continually at odds with the two patent theatres, which in turn did all they could to enforce their monopoly. During the eighteenth century two Acts of Parliament were passed, which, although not defining the position very clearly, in practice enabled the monopoly conditions to continue. The Licensing Act of 1737 gave the Crown, through the Lord Chamberlain, unlimited powers in licence and censorship of plays within the confines of the City of Westminster. Each succeeding Lord Chamberlain interpreted the Act differently, some reading it literally and licensing 'illegitimate' houses, others sustaining the patent theatres to the exclusion of all rivals. A second Act, passed in 1752, extended its scope to all places of amusement in Westminster and elsewhere, and gave authority to local magistrates to grant licences at their quarter sessions. Between the magistrates and the Lord Chamberlain there was only a vague understanding concerning the restriction of licensed theatres to 'illegitimate' drama. No real definition existed as to how far these theatres were confined to pantomime, music, and dancing. A further Act of 1832 merely confirmed previous enactments and extended the powers of local magistrates to license 'legitimate' theatres outside the twenty-mile limit of London. This third Act greatly increased the number of theatres in the provinces, for although in the larger cities theatres already existed under royal patent, magistrates could now license performances of serious drama in any town or city, and companies unable to work in London owing to monopoly conditions found new scope for their activities.

One of the minor theatres had in 1787 defied these monopoly conditions by putting on *As You Like It*, with the result that the patent theatres immediately had the unfortunate manager charged with vagrancy. This was due to the original Licensing Act, which revived the vagrancy law, under which actors performing without a licence were termed " vagrants and sturdy beggars." With the rights of the patent theatres upheld, the minor theatres were confined to presenting dancing, pantomime, and what came to be known as the burletta.

Originally the burletta was a burlesque type of musical piece without a word of dialogue, and when the plot required some explanation too difficult to portray by miming alone large pieces of cloth were lowered from the flies, on which, in letters big enough for all to read, the story was told. The development of the burletta is, in effect, the story of the rise of the minor theatres and the eventual defeat of monopoly. When melodrama was introduced from France, early in the century, it was given a similar form to the burletta, and in the eyes of the law was subject to the same conditions. Elliston was the first manager of the minor theatres to develop the possibilities arising out of the vagueness of the law in defining 'illegitimate' drama. He rented the Royal Circus, later known as the Surrey Theatre, which, like Astley's, had been giving equestrian displays. Under the title of burletta he presented *Macbeth* and other well-known classics. In order to conform with the law and to escape the wrath of the patent theatres Elliston largely rewrote the plays in doggerel verse and arranged a continuous piano accompaniment. This advance on the completely dumb-show kind of entertainment continued, and the important question now arose as to how much music should accompany the speaking of the verse. As time went on the piano accompaniment dwindled until it existed only as a few almost inaudible chords. When Dibdin the song-writer succeeded Elliston at the **Surrey** he presented *The Vicar of Wakefield*, which was highly praised, although one writer regretted that " the good old Vicar is forced to sing in order to evade the watchfulness of the proprietors of the two patent theatres." By this time, in 1819, the definition of 'burletta' came to include a prose comedy, provided it had five songs to each act. The minor theatres usually paid more care and attention to the scenery and costumes than did the patent theatres, who, in order to attract full houses, were nevertheless forced to concentrate more on spectacle than the legitimate drama in which they held the monopoly. Indeed, in 1831, as *The Observer* pointed out, Drury Lane was showing *Timor the Tartar* and the horses, at Covent Garden *The Life and Death of Buonaparte* was showing as a mere spectacle with horses; while, on the other hand, the minors were presenting, at Sadler's Wells, *Romeo and Juliet* and *Katherine and Petruchio*, at the Surrey *Richard III* and other Shakespearean plays, and at the new City Theatre *The Merchant of Venice*. These productions of Shakespeare were arranged to conform with the burletta conditions, but their success emphasized the futility of the prevailing conditions.

In 1832 a group of writers for the stage met under the chairmanship of Bulwer Lytton, and a petition to Parliament followed. The same year a Bill was presented to Parliament whose purpose was to free the minors from the monopoly, and so once more make conditions possible for creative writing for the theatre. The Bill passed the Commons, but was rejected by the Lords, chiefly because of a fanatical speech by the Bishop of London, making an attack on theatres in general, as hot-beds of vice and immorality.

Fortunately for the minors, the Lord Chamberlain at the time, Lord Conyngham, sympathized with them, and interpreted the Licensing Act as a means to extend the interests of the theatre. He granted many licences to new theatres, and extended the seasons of the Adelphi and the Olympic. He also insisted on the patent theatres limiting their performances to spoken dialogue, and made them close during Lent, although the minors were allowed to keep open.

The patent theatres themselves were now running at a loss because of the restrictions on their monopoly, and soon serious drama dwindled in their programmes, eventually disappearing completely. Finally, in 1843, the Theatre Regulations Act was passed, the minors at last acquired their freedom, and theatre monopoly passed into history.

By this time there had been considerable development in the presentation of plays, chiefly due to the activities of the actor-manager, who now dominated the scene. Acting itself greatly developed under new styles created by the leading actors who succeeded Kemble. The first of the new stars was Edmund Kean, who grew up in the theatre and at an early age was a strolling player in the provinces. Making his debut at Drury Lane in 1814 as Shylock, he thrilled the audience with a new style of interpretation, highly emotional and passionate, acting rather by inspiration than in the calm, studied, classical manner of Kemble. His success was immediate, and with a rapidly increasing salary he played all the great tragic rôles of Hamlet, Othello, Macbeth, Lear, and Richard III. He acquired a fortune in his first years in London, but lived rather recklessly, became involved in a scandal, and left England to tour in America. In the rapidly growing Eastern cities theatres were springing up, and English actors, proving very popular, were finding an attractive new field for further increasing their fortunes. Kean was not satisfied with the success he found in America, and eventually he returned to London, appearing at Drury Lane. The public appeared to distinguish the actor from the man, and his reception was as warm as in his most popular days before the scandal. His way of life, however, still estranged him from polite society and exacted its toll; and when, in 1833, he died at forty-six he was an exhausted and a prematurely aged man.

Two years after Edmund Kean made his Drury Lane debut William Charles Macready first appeared at the Covent Garden, then in the last year of Kemble's management. Macready had not the immediate success of Edmund Kean, but proved in the long run to

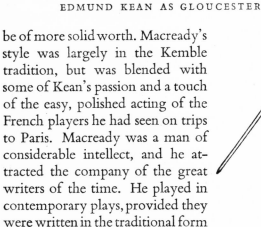

EDMUND KEAN AS GLOUCESTER

be of more solid worth. Macready's style was largely in the Kemble tradition, but was blended with some of Kean's passion and a touch of the easy, polished acting of the French players he had seen on trips to Paris. Macready was a man of considerable intellect, and he attracted the company of the great writers of the time. He played in contemporary plays, provided they were written in the traditional form of comedy or tragedy, but had his greatest successes in Shakespearean parts. A man of good taste, he achieved much in raising the standard of production of serious plays. For the first time since Garrick's day plays received adequate rehearsal. Previously actors had merely read their lines and were allowed at the actual

MACREADY AS HAMLET

performance to interpret their parts as they wished, provided the interpretation was within the bounds of the accepted traditions. Under these conditions a play of Shakespeare's with Edmund Kean resolved itself into the solo performance of the star, surrounded by a host of supernumeraries. Macready, when he was in management, ensured that rehearsals were thorough, that all parts were equally well played, and that the whole production aimed at a unified effect. To attain this end he cast aside the rather mangled forms of Shakespeare's plays that were universally used at the time, and went back to the original text. To ensure that his scenery and costumes were harmonious and correct, he employed J. R. Planché, who, apart from being an accomplished writer of the lighter forms of entertainment, was an expert on historical costumes. Planché had collaborated in 1823 with Charles Kemble, who had succeeded his brother John as manager at Covent Garden, in a production of *King John*, in which, for the first time in the history of the theatre, ancient costumes of the past were reproduced with reasonable accuracy. Macready had periods of management at both the patent theatres during the monopoly period, both of which proved financially unsuccessful. He also played at many of the minor theatres and had many successful tours, including those to America. He retired from the stage in 1851, and died in 1873.

CHARLES KEAN AS HENRY V

In 1827 Charles Kean, the son of Edmund, began acting, much against his father's wish. A limited success started him on a life of touring the provinces and, for some years, America. Having achieved some reputation in America, he returned to London at a convenient time, when Macready was about to retire, and, making full use of the opportunity, soon became the leading tragedian of the day. In 1849 Queen Victoria, who, unlike other monarchs of the previous hundred years, took an interest in the theatre, saw him, and was so delighted with his performance that she inaugurated a series of 'theatricals' at Windsor Castle, with Kean as 'Master of the Revels.' The Queen's regular attendance at the theatre, together with the more scholarly and tasteful productions of Macready and Kean, had the effect of bringing back the upper classes into the auditorium.

Charles Kean had not the brilliant, though erratic, genius of his father, and was generally considered to be a lesser actor, but as a manager he saw to it that he was surrounded by a first-rate cast, and that his productions were mounted with taste and splendour. He continued with Macready's ideas of using historically accurate costumes and of working out the production in detail so that no longer did the leading actor monopolize the stage and by over-

emphasis distort the true intent of the play. Kean took over management of the Princess's Theatre in 1850, and enjoyed continual success for nine years, after which he played in the provinces and undertook extensive tours of America and Australia. This small theatre made possible the long run. Previously only the spec-
tacular after-pieces and pantomimes ever enjoyed runs of several weeks. Plays were continued only as long as the public would attend, and during the first half of the century a fortnight was the usual length of run for serious drama, although, of course, the production could be judiciously re-vived from time to time. Kean's productions at the Princess's usually ran for a hundred nights. Apart from his Shakespearean successes, Kean was responsible for the introduction of contemporary French dramas on the London stage.

What Charles Kean and Macready did for the production of serious drama Madame Vestris and C. J. Matthews did for comedy and burlesque. Vestris, a charming and delightful creature pos-sessed of a rich contralto voice, married a famous ballet-master, Armand Vestris, only to be separated a few years later. Although she was by profession a dancer, her first London appearance in 1815 was as an opera singer, and she subsequently appeared at the patent theatres as singer, dancer, and actress, acquiring great popularity as a personality. It is her achievements as a manager, however, which make her position important in the early Victorian theatre. In 1831 she acquired the management of the small Olympic Theatre, at which she intended to present 'legitimate' drama, but in accordance

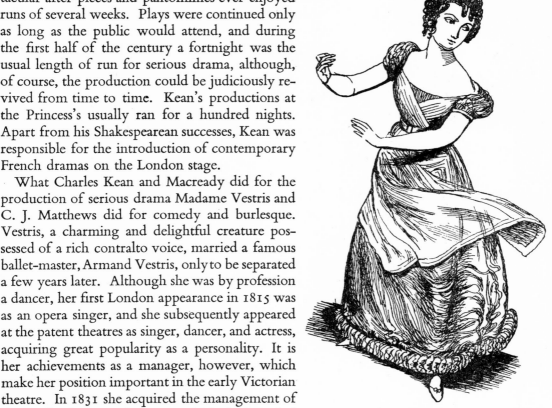

MADAME VESTRIS IN "PAUL PRY"

with the current, monopoly conditions. The little theatre was redecorated in the prevailing excellent taste and made much more comfortable than the large patent theatres.

In many ways the Olympic was the forerunner of the small intimate theatres which are to be found in London to-day. It presented comedies and burlesques by J. R. Planché and others, and in the manner of presentation achieved a quiet revolution. For some years past characters in comedies had always worn eccentric costumes, and comic acting was broad and extravagant. Madame Vestris introduced the use of contemporary costume, and when we consider that the period from 1830 to 1850 was probably the most charming, from the point of view of costume, in the whole century, it can well be imagined that the productions reached new heights of taste and elegance. Her company was a small one and chosen with care. None of her productions required a large cast, and consequently a high standard of acting was achieved in all parts. By this time stalls were being introduced into the pit, and gradually the fashionable element of society began to frequent theatres again. The intimate atmosphere of the Olympic appealed to them, particularly when they could be assured of a refined and tasteful production. Madame Vestris made the innovation of concluding the evening's programme by about eleven o'clock; before this the theatres rarely concluded their performances before midnight, and when the bill was particularly long they went on until the small hours of the morning.

C. J. MATTHEWS IN A LIGHT-
COMEDY RÔLE

Charles Matthews the younger joined the company in 1835, and rapidly became the leading light comedian of the day. His father, the elder Charles Matthews, had been a famous comic actor, known chiefly for his monologues and character studies. Matthews was sympathetic to the policy of his manager, and developed a style of acting based on the observation of contemporary manners. He soon succumbed to the charms of Madame Vestris, and married her three years later. Not long after their marriage they gave up the Olympic and spent a year touring in America. On their return to London they took over management of Covent Garden, but because of the general monopoly conditions they were not very successful. During their management there a further milestone was passed in the great trend towards realism which was the century's contribution to theatrical art, for in 1841 a play by Dion Boucicault called *London Assurance* was produced. Boucicault was an actor and writer with a thorough knowledge of both French and English stage traditions, and while chiefly engaged in adapting French pieces for the English stage, he was feeling his way in the quest of a more realistic contemporary drama. He later developed a more melodramatic style.

In spite of some excellent productions of Shakespeare's comedies, the Vestris-Matthews management at Covent Garden ceased in 1842, and after a few years of various managements they acquired control of the Lyceum, where they went back to burlesque and light comedy. This was their last management together, Madame Vestris retiring in 1854 and dying two years later, although Matthews continued acting for another twenty years.

Contemporaneous with Charles Kean's management of the Princess's Theatre was Samuel Phelps's management of Sadler's Wells. Phelps, who had received his training under Macready, in 1844 took over management of this theatre, which previously had confined its activities to melodrama, and, making use of its watery surroundings, had a large tank

PHELPS AS FALSTAFF

on the stage for aquatic displays. Sadler's Wells had generally a low reputation as a rendezvous for the rougher elements in the town. And yet Phelps played Shakespeare there successfully for eighteen years, during which most of Shakespeare's plays were produced, in addition to other classic dramas of the past. His own acting was in the Macready style, and he shone particularly as Falstaff and Malvolio. In contrast to Charles Kean, he stressed good acting, settings and costumes having less importance in his productions. His great success was possibly due partly to the fact that this was the first time that serious drama had been given at this theatre, which had hitherto suffered from a surfeit of spectacle and watery melodrama.

By the middle of the century there had been considerable development in the theatre since Kemble's time. The early years of the monopoly period were great times for the scenic artist. Settings of romantic grandeur played an important part in burletta and melodrama, artists designing not only interiors but whole landscapes. The scenery became more solid and built-up, and the constant change of scene that was required demanded some development in stage machinery. As settings became more elaborate the stage roof was heightened to enable the scenery to be hoisted up out of sight of the audience. Devices such as the diorama were evolved. The diorama was a landscape painted on a continuous backcloth, which, mounted on rollers and turned mechanically, gave the audience some illusion of movement in plays where exciting journeys or races took place. The use of the apron stage, when there was one, declined as the action of the play was developed behind the proscenium. The cumbersome scenery now still further confined the acting space. Although Kean had developed historical accuracy in costume and setting, scenery was still artificial in the sense that it was chiefly painted scenery and not three-dimensional. Interiors, for instance, were still represented by a painted backcloth and several sets of wings, while the ceiling was represented by a hanging border.

Gas-lighting had been introduced early in the century, being used originally to light the auditorium, and was gradually developed for stage purposes. The great advantage of gas-lighting was in its control. The days of the 'invisible' candle-snuffer now belonged to history, and with the movement of a lever a stage mechanic could subdue or increase the lighting at will. In 1860 the first use was made of limelight, which produced a strong, incandescent light, and became the chief means of emphasizing a character, or portion of a scene. The limelight led to the use of incandescent gas-lighting, which greatly increased its effectiveness.

By this time there had come about a great change in the auditorium of the theatre. Upholstered seats were now provided in the boxes and the stalls, which were gradually ousting the pit to the rear of the theatre. The crudely printed play-bills, a foot or more in length, and printed in ink that smeared at a touch, had given way to smaller, better-printed programmes, much the same as those we know to-day. Following the interest of the Queen, polite society was back in the theatre. These factors, together with the fact that the novelty of the new technical advances on the stage had been played out, combined to bring about a desire for some development of drama itself in a new direction. A step in this new direction was achieved under the management of Charles Fechter, a well-known French actor who had first appeared in London acting at the St James's Theatre in French plays. French companies had always made periodic visits to London, usually playing at the Queen's, the Lyceum, or the St James's. Mlle Rachel had acted at the St James's and had attracted the fashionable world much as Sarah Bernhardt was to do later. In 1860 Fechter appeared at the Princess's in *Ruy Blas* and later as Hamlet, playing in English. It was in *Hamlet* that Fechter created a sensation, not only in acting but also in production. In contrast to the traditional English style of tragic acting, he played the rôle in a comparatively realistic manner, interpreting the play as a refined melodrama. Fechter was the innovator of the box set, an interior setting with the appearance of solid walls and with a realistic ceiling. He also used a sinking stage, so that all the solidly built scenery could be changed in the basement.

Five years later a new management made its contribution to the rapidly changing methods

FECHTER AS HAMLET

of stage representation. Marie Wilton, who had succeeded Vestris as queen of burlesque, went into partnership with H. J. Byron, a writer of light pieces, at the old Prince of Wales's Theatre, the site of which is now occupied by the Scala. It soon became noted for its production of a new kind of play, by a rising young dramatist, Tom Robertson. He had already won recognition with *David Garrick* at the Haymarket, in which the famous E. A. Sothern had appeared with great success. Robertson's subsequent plays, *Society*, *Ours*, *Caste*, *M.P.*, *Play*, and *School*, were all comedy-dramas, based on contemporary life, with flesh-and-blood characters drawn from observation of life of the times. Marie Wilton acted in these plays with Squire Bancroft, whom she soon married, and John Hare. The Bancrofts further

H

developed the realistic method of production which had begun with Fechter, and which Robertson had visualized for his plays. Scenery became thoroughly realistic, much of the painted architectural detail of interior sets giving way to solid cornices and pillars. Furniture acquired a new dramatic significance, and the Bancrofts spent much time and trouble in creating a realistic atmosphere regarding general detail. In *Money*, by Lord Lytton, an exact reproduction was made on the stage of a card-room in a famous West End club.

Robertson had been an actor, and he knew the problems of the stage. His realism was, of course, only comparative; to-day his plays seem stagey and melodramatic, but at the time they were written they gave the public a new representation of mid-Victorian life with all its social and economic significance. His work made possible the portrayal of social problems on the stage, which were further developed by Pinero, Henry Arthur Jones, and later by Galsworthy. In Pinero's *Trelawney of the Wells* the character of Tom Wrench is supposed to be Robertson in his early days. The play is also interesting for its portrayal of stage life and the changing conditions of the times.

The Bancrofts had twenty years of unbroken success, having finally moved to the Haymarket in 1879. They were responsible for many innovations in management, notably the restriction of the programme to one play, the raising of the status of the small-part player, and the introduction of the matinee performance.

At the time of the Bancrofts' management the music-halls reached new heights of importance. Originally the halls were special saloons attached to a tavern, where musical entertainment as well as refreshment was provided. With the passing of the Theatre Regulations Act of 1843 and the abolition of monopoly, plays could be given at any licensed house, but no smoking or drinking was allowed in the auditorium. This was permitted, however, at the music-halls, and by 1870 there were over twenty of them in London; some were quite large theatres, such as the Alhambra, and in the eighties many palatial new theatres were built, including the Empire and the New Tivoli. The audiences consisted chiefly of the working class and the male section of the middle class, and the fare provided was fashioned to suit their demands. The artists had only to amuse and entertain, with no pretensions to art; they knew what their audiences wanted, and if they could provide it well enough they were assured of success. The best of them assumed set characters, in which they invariably appeared, usually with a rather eccentric costume and make-up. Their brief turn on the stage was made up of song, dance, and comic patter. Acrobats, jugglers, and contortionists also found their place on the programme. The stars were able to play at several theatres during the evening, repeating their short turn at each and driving off to the next theatre. Their songs still live to-day—that is, the tunes are still heard, but the words usually seem either vulgar or trite. The songs were specially written for the working-class audience of those times, and in them is often reflected their social and economic discontent. Such stars as Jenny Hill, Dan Leno, Alfred Glanville Vance, George Leybourne, Herbert Campbell, Albert Chevalier, Gus Elen, Vesta Tilley, and Marie Lloyd had immense popularity, and attracted crowded houses to the music-halls, or the variety theatres, as they came to be known. The rougher elements of the town, who in the past made the ' O.P.' riots possible, had by now largely deserted the theatres in favour of the variety houses. The theatres had almost become the sole domain of the middle class. However, theatres such as Drury Lane, with their thousands of seats to be filled, could not afford to ignore the drawing-power of the variety stars, and therefore engaged them to fill the chief parts in their annual panto-mimes. Whatever the pantomime was, the stars had little to do, apart from their normal music-hall turn. The Christmas pantomime to-day still makes use of variety stars to fill the chief parts, although in the last few years players from the legitimate stage have been included.

From the time of the Bancrofts' production of Robertson's plays onward the tendency of stage presentation became increasingly realistic. With the introduction of electric lighting at the Savoy in 1880, a great step forward had been made. The great flexibility and control of electricity made all kinds of realistic effects possible for the first time. It was now possible to reproduce the effect of sunlight, and outside settings could be made more realistic, while a subdued lighting effect was just as simple to create. Stage equipment and machinery were improved to enable an easier change of scene. From Germany, where the technical improve-ments of the stage were chiefly developed, came the sliding and sinking stages, which enabled whole settings to be moved out of sight and replaced with an entirely complete scene, the cyclorama, the revolving stage, and many electrical devices for controlling lighting. The cyclorama in Germany was developed as a plaster half-dome covering the back of the stage, on which light could be thrown to represent the sky. Since it had no shadows it gave a great illusion of depth, particularly if a blue light was used. The cyclorama reached England in a different form, as a sky-cloth of canvas hung in a large semicircular arc, which could be drawn to one side if necessary. The large stages of Covent Garden and Drury Lane were reconstructed in sections, each of which could be raised or lowered at will, enabling built-up scenic effects to be quickly changed.

Actors, too, were developing their technique, throwing aside many traditional habits of stagey presentation. The greatest figure of the last thirty years of the century was Henry Irving. Like many actors before him, he served his apprenticeship in his art in the provincial theatres of Dublin, Liverpool, Manchester, and other big cities, and by the time he made his London debut, in 1866, he was an experienced and accomplished actor. His performance as Hamlet in 1874 established his reputation as the leading actor on the English stage. By comparison with the tragic actors of the past, he gave a fresh and naturalistic interpretation, and his use of the new improvements in the theatre as they became available ensured his continual success. One of his innovations was the stage black-out, during which scenery was changed. Irving had a wonderful sense of the pictorial effect of a scene. He managed to interest some of the leading painters in designing for the stage, and persuaded Burne-Jones, Alma-Tadema, Ford Madox Brown, and Gustave Doré to work for him. Some of his productions tended towards over-elaboration, as he was in the habit of introducing con-siderable stage business not in the script. Apart from Shakespeare, Irving preferred to use rather inferior plays and adaptations as vehicles for his art. It seems a pity that great acting should be remembered chiefly by the production of quite second-rate plays. He economized on authors in this way, and was able to spend more on production. In spite of this economy, after long periods of management at the Lyceum Irving failed financially, and in 1899 the management was taken over by a syndicate.

As an actor, a personality, and a man, Irving was always looked up to, and he did much to raise the status of the acting profession. He became the first actor to receive the honour of a knighthood. He played in melodrama, and is particularly remembered for his performance

IRVING AS MATHIAS IN "THE BELLS"

in the horror-play *The Bells*. He possessed enormous personal magnetism, and held audiences spell-bound by the mastery of his acting. His style was not a passionate one, but by superb timing his long speeches moved the audience much as they had been moved by Garrick. His popularity was also great in America, where he made many tours. His last tour was begun in England in 1905, and he died in Bradford a few days after. He was buried in Westminster Abbey.

Ellen Terry was the leading actress during the last quarter of the century. She was born of parents who were well-known provincial actors and close friends of Charles Kean. She first appeared on the stage in 1856 at an early age as the boy Mamillius in *The Winter's Tale* at the Princess Theatre. In 1867 she played with Irving as Katherine to his Petruchio in *The Taming of the Shrew*. For some years after this she retired from the stage, returning in 1875, when she played Portia under the Bancrofts' management at the old Prince of Wales. After this she rejoined Irving, and a long and happy partnership ensued in which she played all Shakespeare's great heroines. Later she also played in some of the early Shaw plays. Most critics of the time write of the freshness and vitality of her acting. Even in her old age she could convincingly portray the feeling of youth.

Lily Langtry was famed more for her beauty and personality than for her acting. She appeared chiefly in modern plays, and achieved tremendous popularity.

The dynamic personality and temperament of Mrs Patrick Campbell accounted for her being much sought after as leading lady. She achieved great success in 1893 in Pinero's very popular *The Second Mrs Tanqueray*. She is particularly remembered as the original Eliza Doolittle in Shaw's *Pygmalion*.

The last years of the century were dominated by the actor-manager, who led his company on the numerous tours that were necessary to ensure a regular living. Each company had its repertoire of plays, to which it was constantly adding, and when playing for a week at a certain town could easily present a fresh play on each evening. For the younger actors who were employed for the tour the variety of parts to be played, which often entailed doubling during the evening, gave good groundwork for developing the powers of acting, and there was no time for their work to become dull and lifeless. The actor-manager usually played the leading rôles himself, but also kept an eye on the performance of the youngsters and gave them their chance when they were ready for it. Most of the managers of the West End theatres in London had been actors at one time and understood the stage. George Alexander, who had acted with Irving, was a typical example. He managed the St James's Theatre, and presented a series of well-produced modern plays by H. A. Jones, Pinero, and Oscar Wilde, with a distinguished company, including Mrs Patrick Campbell, Irene Vanbrugh, Marie Tempest, and Henry Ainley.

Herbert Beerbohm Tree was chiefly known for his melodramatic and character parts, Falstaff and Hamlet being his most successful rôles. In his productions of Shakespeare he was greatly influenced by Irving's elaboration of the stage picture. He founded a school for acting, and was prominent in furthering the interests of the theatre.

Frank Benson led a company which included most of Shakespeare's plays in their repertoire. They travelled all over the country, and as far as Canada and South Africa. For many years Benson organized the annual festivals at Stratford-on-Avon. His organization of a regular touring company was superb, and he had considerable influence on his contemporaries. His company were almost as well known for their cricket prowess as for their acting, and it is said that he recruited the men of his company with more thought for their skill at the wicket than their ability on the boards.

Johnston Forbes-Robertson served his apprenticeship with Samuel Phelps. He played under the Bancrofts' management, and at various times with Irving. He took up management at the Lyceum in 1895. His distinguished appearance and romantic temperament suited him in his best parts—Romeo, Hamlet, and Macbeth. Other actor-managers who achieved distinction in their work were Charles Wyndham, Wilson Barrett, John Martin-Harvey, Cyril Maude, Charles Hawtrey, and Arthur Bourchier.

The century had seen great technical development in the theatre. Acting ability had progressed along more individual paths; no longer was there a conventional style, but the trend had been generally to more and more realism. Until the end of the century few plays of lasting value were written, and now it was to drama itself that the world looked for further development.

# CHAPTER EIGHT

# The Russians and Our Theatre

*Plate VIII*

---

*A Surrealist "Orestes"*

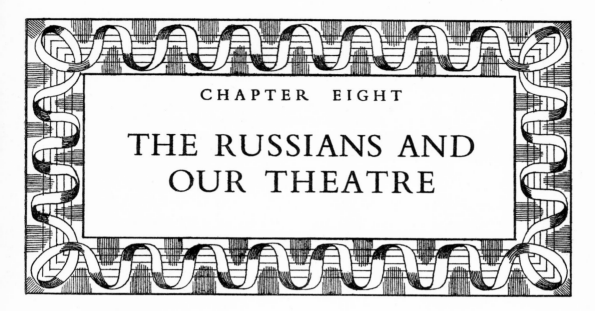

# CHAPTER EIGHT

# THE RUSSIANS AND OUR THEATRE

TOWARDS THE END OF THE NINETEENTH CENTURY there arose, among a certain section of theatre-goers, a feeling of dissatisfaction with the state of things in the theatre. This dissatisfaction showed itself in the formation, in most European countries, of small groups of individuals who joined together in a common purpose to encourage writers and producers of contemporary plays that normally would not be produced in the established theatres. The realism which the theatre had achieved during the century was still a stagey realism, and to many people was a disappointment. To most of the dissentient groups the actor-manager system of production, with its inevitable emphasis on leading rôles, was quite unacceptable.

In England a group was formed by J. T. Grein with the purpose of producing, at a series of semi-private performances, Continental and British plays which would not otherwise see production on the popular stage. In 1891 Ibsen's *Ghosts* was first produced in England by Grein's Independent Theatre Group, which later became the Stage Society. Ibsen was primarily a poet and secondly a fine stage craftsman. His early works were chiefly poetical dramas on rather vague and mystical themes, *Peer Gynt* being the most important. He had been connected with the theatre in Norway for most of his life, and not until the age of fifty did he begin writing the great prose dramas to which he owes his reputation outside his own country. *Ghosts*, his second prose drama, has as its main theme the struggle of the individual against society. Its performance in England created quite a stir, some people reacting against the rather depressing picture it presented, others seeing the lyrical qualities flowing through the intensely real characters while they are involved in their own internal struggles. Ibsen was superb at creating characters, and all his plays stress the supreme importance of individual personality. His characters are all real people, with human traits and weaknesses, and whether the action takes place in the house of a doctor, a town councillor, or a master-builder, in surroundings of matter-of-fact realism, through the cleverly constructed dialogue the poetical qualities of the play will always emerge.

The production of *Ghosts* was followed by other plays by Continental authors, and in 1892 by George Bernard Shaw's first play, *Widowers' Houses*. By 1899, when it became the Stage Society, the Independent Theatre had presented twenty-six new plays, all of which had some intellectual claim to performance. The group was made up of less than two hundred subscribers, but they included actors, critics, writers for the theatre, and many distinguished people. By the introduction of these brilliant plays, continuing under the Stage Society, which produced plays by Ibsen, Gorky, Maeterlinck, Hauptmann, Brieux, Shaw, Strindberg, Barker, and Yeats, the foundation was laid for the development of intellectual drama in the twentieth century.

In 1897 two men met at a restaurant in Moscow to discuss the formation of a new theatre. They were Vladimir Nemirovitch-Dantchenko and Constantin Stanislavsky. Dantchenko at forty was playwright, critic, and producer, and at that time was director of the Philharmonic, one of the two dramatic academies in Moscow. Stanislavsky was a well-to-do merchant of thirty-six, who some years previously had formed a group of actors, all amateurs, in order to produce interesting and unusual plays. Both men were dissatisfied with conditions in the theatres at that time, both had ideas about the way in which plays should be produced, and together with Dantchenko's students and Stanislavsky's amateurs, they had the nucleus of a permanent company. When they had finally agreed on the organization of the theatre they set about raising the necessary funds. This was found to be difficult until an eccentric million-aire merchant named Morozov provided them with the greater part of the money required. They acquired a small theatre in Moscow, and called it the Moscow Art Theatre. Stanis-lavsky was to have charge of the artistic policy and actual direction of the productions, while Dantchenko was to choose the plays and control the administration of the theatre. A whole year was spent in preparation for the opening, in welding the two groups together, and in rehearsing a repertoire of several plays. The policy of the new theatre was to produce plays of distinction by Russian and foreign writers, to subordinate individual acting to the idea of the play itself, to pay great attention to detail and also to characterization, and to avoid completely the conventional staginess current in the other theatres of the time. Stanislavsky was a good actor himself, and he appeared in many leading parts ; he was also a great director, with a will of iron, and with infinite patience he worked at rehearsals throughout the summer of 1898, the rehearsals being held in a barn in the country just outside Moscow.

The method of rehearsal of plays had hitherto been a summary one. The actors would arrive on the stage, be presented with a copy of their parts, and would immediately begin to read their lines and walk about the stage, taking up various 'effective' positions. The whole play would be gone through at each rehearsal until the actors were word-perfect, when the play was considered ready for the first performance. The producer suggested their moves on the stage, which, if found convenient, were adopted, without thought to the dramatic significance of those moves. Often the stars would disagree with the producer, whose authority was little higher than that of a stage-manager, and on these occasions he would have to give way. Stanislavsky's methods were quite different. In the first place, there were no stars in the Art Theatre, and all the players were submitted to the most rigid discipline from the director. Rehearsals of a new play would begin, not on the stage, but in the comfort of a private room. This would take the form of a discussion on the play, in which the director and whole cast would thrash out their ideas of the play and how the various parts should be played. Sometimes the discussion would take place with the author present to explain his ideas of the play. Not until the play had been read and thoroughly understood by all the cast did actual rehearsals begin. Stanislavsky rehearsed only a small part of the play at one rehearsal—perhaps only one scene, which would be gone over several times until the actors had found the right cadence of voice, or the right movements, which

NEMIROVITCH-DANTCHENKO

STANISLAVSKY

Stanislavsky had pictured for the characterization. So by rehearsing a scene, or a fragment of a scene, at a time, the whole play would be built up by a concentration of effort on minute detail, and by the help of the underlying conception of how the characters would act in real life. In the other theatres of the time a dress rehearsal was not considered necessary. The players had their own wardrobe, and wore what they pleased, often without even consulting the director. The actresses decided what gowns to wear by mutual arrangement, so that there should not be a clash of colour. Stanislavsky held five or six dress rehearsals of the entire play, and many more of fragments of the play, with leading actors in costume and make-up, and with the appropriate scenery. These dress rehearsals of parts of the play took place two months before the final dress rehearsals.

Another principle of the Art Theatre was that each play should have its own setting, specially designed to suit the theme and mood of the play. This does not seem an outrageous demand at the present day, but in those times the theatres usually had a stock of scenery, a drawing-room set, a wood set, and so on, and whatever the setting of the play this scenery was used. The management of these theatres having never conceived the idea of attracting artists into the theatre to design the settings, the scenery was painted by a decorator, a kind of superior stage-hand.

The first production at the opening of the theatre in October 1898 was Tolstoy's *Tsar Feodor*, which was followed by Shakespeare's *Merchant of Venice*, two plays by Goldoni, a modern Russian play by Pisemsky, *The Sunken Bell*, by Hauptmann, *Antigone*, by Sophocles, *Hedda Gabler*, by Ibsen, and *The Seagull*, by Chekhov. These plays became part of the permanent repertoire as they were presented, and were repeated alternately from time to time. Thus the actors did not have the boring task of playing the same part every night, but had a variety of parts, and occasionally no part, which ensured one or two free evenings during the week.

The debut of the new theatre received appreciative response from public and Press, and though the audiences fell off a little after the opening, the production of Chekhov's *The Seagull* ensured the ultimate success of the company. *The Seagull* had been produced at one of the Imperial theatres at St Petersburg two years previously, and had been a complete failure. Chekhov was a doctor who had taken to writing short stories of typical Russian life, which brought fame and literary distinction in the award of an Academy prize. He then wrote two one-act farces, vaudeville pieces, as he called them—*The Bear* and *The Proposal* —which were successful everywhere. These were followed by *Ivanov*, which achieved only moderate success at a performance in a private theatre. *The Seagull* was his first great play, but although he attended the rehearsals at St Petersburg, the actors could make nothing of it. Chekhov had offered the play to the Moscow Small Theatre, the most advanced of the established theatres, but Lensky, the leading actor, had returned the play, advising Chekhov to give up writing for the stage. Chekhov represented human beings as he observed them in life, and his training as a doctor made his characterization extremely penetrating. His characters are inseparable from their own particular surroundings, and his plays are full of atmosphere; merged with his dialogue are the sounds of neighbours arriving at the house, the samovar, the rain, and the soft playing of guitar or piano. It can be understood that the actors of the old school, with their staginess of technique and their conventional style, could not hope to portray the author's conception of character and mood. After its failure Chekhov resolved to write no more for the theatre, but two years later Dantchenko persuaded him to let the Art Theatre produce the play.

Stanislavsky's rejection of the old conventional style of acting, in which the player acted set emotions, words, or situations, and his concentration on the individual character by awakening the feelings that the particular character experienced, gave Chekhov the first possibility of a competent interpretation. Only by naturalistic acting can Chekhov's plays seem convincing; with stagey acting the dialogue seems ridiculous. In his intricate building up of detail to create atmosphere Stanislavsky sometimes went to extremes. Thus in *Uncle Vanya*, which was produced a year later, mosquito-nets appeared on the heads of some of the characters, and the sound of a cricket chirping was heard from behind the stove. Stanislavsky's production was always theatrical, but not stagey, in that it was real life he reproduced on the stage, but reality enlarged. In historical plays, for instance, if high hats had been worn in the period presented the characters' hats were made even higher, if long sleeves were worn they would be so long that they had to be tucked in, while if a door was to be small it was made so small that the actors had to bend double to pass through. Stanislavsky had not Chekhov's knowledge of the provincial Russian intelligentsia of the time, with its loves, its tears, its envies, and its quarrels, but he successfully reproduced it on the stage. The greatness of Chekhov is in the lyrical qualities of his plays, which always emerge through the everyday realities of his provincial households.

The Art Theatre developed a more naturalistic method of lighting, using much greater variation than was usually thought possible, at times even having so little light on the actors that they were hardly discernible. As designer, a painter of the Russian realistic school,

SETTING FOR "THE THREE SISTERS" (ACT I) AT THE MOSCOW ART THEATRE

Simov, was brought in to design the settings. He entered into the task with great enthusiasm, which was matched only by his achievements. Dantchenko, in his book *My Life in the Russian Theatre*, writes of a child in the audience at a performance of *The Seagull* who turned to its parent and said, " Mother, let's go into the garden for a walk."

Although the first season showed a loss, the enthusiastic Morozov made good the loss, and the other shareholders followed suit, so that the theatre was safe for the next season. The following season other plays by Hauptmann, Tolstoy, and Shakespeare, together with Chekhov's *Uncle Vanya*, were added to the repertoire. The Art Theatre now gained considerable reputation and began to make its influence felt in the other theatres. In 1901 Chekhov's *Three Sisters*, which had been specially written for the actors at the Art Theatre, was produced there. This is considered their finest production. His *Cherry Orchard* was produced in the spring of 1904, and in the summer of that year he died on a holiday in Germany. In Chekhov's plays we can sense his awareness of the decay and futility of Russian life among the upper classes, and it is fascinating to speculate what effects the tremendous events of 1917 might have had on his writing for the theatre.

Another great writer whose work was produced at the Art Theatre was Maxim Gorky. His plays, dealing in a starkly realistic manner with low life in the vast interior of Russia, could only have been produced at the Art Theatre.

The Moscow Art Theatre was not confined entirely to naturalistic production, and in the production of Maeterlinck's *Blue Bird* the naturalistic element was entirely subordinated to a spirit of pure fantasy. Also, in 1911 Gordon Craig produced *Hamlet* for the Art Theatre, but in his own unique style. Gordon Craig, the son of Ellen Terry, had begun his career acting in Irving's company. After two or three years, deciding that he could no longer continue as part of a system for which he had no sympathy, he resigned from a well-paid position in order to formulate his own conception of the production of plays and the way the theatre should be organized. He evolved ideas which were so revolutionary at that time that he could find no outlet for his work, and he was compelled, in order to make a living, to write and publish his ideas, and to make designs for settings, chiefly through the medium of woodcuts. His chief objection to contemporary staging lay in the fact that on the stage the actors were three-dimensional flesh-and-blood characters who reproduced the story of the play, while the scenery merely served as a background, and was largely two-dimensional. Craig conceived a bigger function for the setting; as with the actors, it should be three-dimensional, and it should play an integral part in the telling of the story or the portraying of the mood of the play. In other words, the scenery should be made to act in co-ordination with the players. He designed settings which were composed chiefly of simple abstract forms, stairways, rostrums, blocks, and cubes, the whole effect presenting a great variety of planes. By throwing various kinds of coloured lighting on the surface of these planes, and arranging the lighting to come from different angles, he was able to achieve an appearance of change and movement, although the actual setting remained static. The actors'

COSTUME FOR "BREAD" FROM THE MOSCOW ART THEATRE'S PRODUCTION OF "THE BLUE BIRD"

position on the stage was worked out as a part of the complete setting, so that actors and scenery, both three-dimensional, formed an integral whole. The scene-painter, with years of development in representing a three-dimensional effect in two dimensions, was rejected by Craig as an anachronism. Craig's settings were usually painted in a neutral colour, and lighting was the sole means of producing coloured effects. Craig was the first man to understand the tremendous value of shadows in producing dramatic effect. His method meant, of course, the entire subordination of the actor to the will of the director's mind, for the latter would conceive the dramatic idea of the play, design the setting, arrange the lighting, and dictate the movement and speech of the actors. In those days in England, when the actor-manager was supreme, Craig found no enthusiasm for his ideas, and he has never been able to run a theatre in England. He went to Italy to live, where he had an opportunity to study the theatre of the past and to develop his ideas further. He published a periodical called *The Mask* for many years in order to propagate his ideas, and, incidentally, to earn a living. He started a dramatic school which unfortunately came to an end during the First World War. His writing and woodcut designs, however, found their way all over Europe, and his influence has been great, particularly in Germany, although in this country he has had little influence, being regarded primarily as a scenic designer, and secondly as a graphic artist. In Germany Adolphe Appia developed along similar lines to Craig, and was particularly noted for his staging of Wagner's operas.

In his formal production of *Hamlet* at Moscow Craig used a series of screens, which could be placed in a variety of positions, thus creating a complete change in the shape of the scene

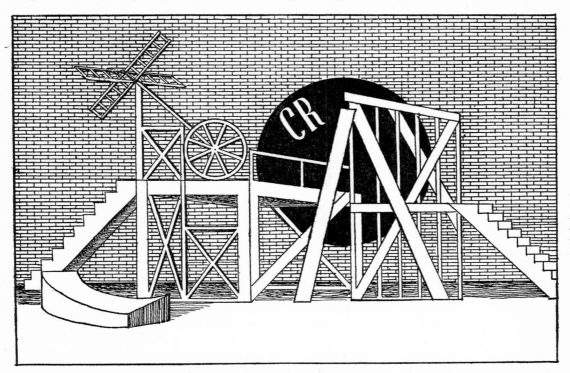

EARLY CONSTRUCTIVIST SETTING FOR A MEYERHOLD PRODUCTION

with very little actual movement. His work there, however, was considered to be little more than a novelty, and the Art Theatre remained a stronghold of naturalistic representation. What both Craig's system and Stanislavsky's had in common was the unity in the various elements of production imposed by the director with strict discipline on actors and technicians of the theatre.

By this time the Art Theatre was firmly established, and it had produced some fine actors apart from Stanislavsky, including Katchalov, Luzhsky, Gribunin, and Moskvin. The actresses never reached the heights of achievement of the men, but those who stood out were Knipper, who married Chekhov, Stanislavsky's wife, Marie Lilina, Germanova, Zhdanova, and Butova. Other theatres began to revolutionize their productions, sometimes in an entirely new direction.

Meyerhold was probably the first and most important director to break away from the Art Theatre's naturalism. He was originally one of Dantchenko's most promising students at his dramatic academy, the Philharmonic, and when the Art Theatre was founded he played in the early productions, notably as Trepleiff in *The Seagull* and as the Baron in *The Three Sisters*. Although an accomplished actor, his ambition was to direct, and after a few years with the Art Theatre he left to direct productions at the theatre of Vera Komisarjevskaya, a noted actress of the time. Her brother, who was also developing his powers as a director there, was later to have his own theatre, after the Revolution, and subsequently came to England and America to work as a director. After a short period at this theatre Meyerhold became director at the two Imperial theatres in St Petersburg, the Alexandrinsky and the

CUBIST PAINTERS BROKE DOWN NATURAL
FORMS TO SIMPLE GEOMETRIC SHAPES

Marinsky. Meyerhold was never satisfied with the intimate atmosphere of the Art Theatre, nor with the policy of naturalistic representation. In a way his ideals were more in keeping with the Elizabethan stage. He rejected the conventional stage picture seen by the audience through the 'picture-frame' of the proscenium arch, and he wanted the audience to be much closer to the actors and to play more than the passive part of merely watching the performance. Meyerhold regarded the audience as an integral part of the performance. At first he swept away the footlights and curtain in the large Imperial theatres, and brought back the apron stage. Scenery was largely dispensed with, the bare wall at the back of the stage becoming visible to the audience, and ramps were constructed to lead from the stage to the auditorium. The plays presented were chiefly the classics, but the scripts were completely re-edited by Meyerhold, who adopted a kind of film technique in cutting them up into a series of short episodes. Later, after the Revolution, when there were more contemporary plays dealing with the recent upheaval of social forces, Meyerhold introduced crowd scenes, with the actors in ordinary day-clothes and without make-up, thus being indistinguishable from the audience. He also developed the use of abstract settings and was influenced by the recent developments in pictorial art known as cubism. Cubism was a method of representing natural shapes and forms in a geometrical manner; thus a portrait head or a landscape was simplified into an arrangement of cubes or box-like shapes, together with spheres and other regular forms. It really arose from the period of experiment in the development of painting when the problem of representing the third dimension, depth, was being explored in a new direction.

As with Craig's ideas, Meyerhold's abstract scenery was an attempt to break away from the conventional method of painted scenery which presented a flat background to the solid

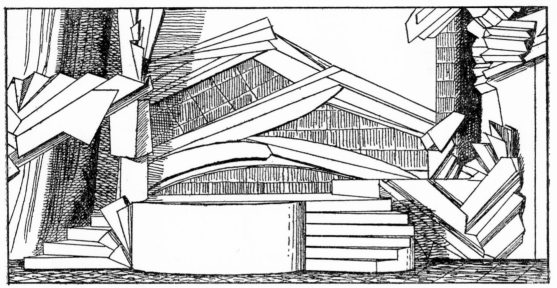

SETTING FOR "ROMEO AND JULIET" AT THE KAMERNY THEATRE DESIGNED BY ALEXANDRA EXTER, SHOWING CUBIST INFLUENCE

figures of the actors. Like Craig, he designed his settings in three dimensions, with the actors as an integral part. Immediately after the Revolution a further development in abstract scenery was what has come to be known as constructivism. This was, as Komisarjevsky points out, partly thrust upon the theatres of the Revolution by the shortage of canvas in the early days of the young Soviet State. A constructivist setting was non-naturalistic, and consisted of an arrangement of wooden platforms, ladders, steps, and gangways, built as a unit, and giving the actors a great variety of levels, angles, and positions from which they could perform. In one play Meyerhold had only the wooden framework of a house, while in others there was considerable ingenuity displayed in arranging the various platforms, ladders, and gangways into a pleasing geometrical design, which had the workmanlike effect of some piece of constructional engineering. Other theatres at this time used constructivist settings, necessity becoming the mother of a new and exciting method of staging. It is obvious that the style of acting had to be adapted to these new surroundings; naturalistic acting would have made the settings appear ridiculous, and so it became more acrobatic and staccato in style. The theatres in Russia eventually returned to more normal methods of staging as conditions became easier, and although naturalistic presentation is more customary at present, the abstract and constructivist period was useful in clearing away many outmoded and conventional ideas in the theatre. It made possible a new and more balanced conception of the values of the various elements in the theatre, and emphasized the need for a universal and more elastic use of the stage.

Another experimental theatre was the Kamerny Theatre, which, under its director, Tairov, produced drama, comedy, pantomime, and light opera. The presentation was frankly

COSTUME FOR "LA PRIN-
CESSE BRAMBILLE" AT
THE KAMERNY THEATRE

COSTUME FOR A MEYER-
HOLD CONSTRUCTIVIST
PRODUCTION

COSTUME FOR "ROMEO AND
JULIET" AT THE KAMERNY
THEATRE

artificial compared with the Art Theatre's realism, and while using no particular stage form, each production having a setting particularly suited to it, it generally moved in the direction of abstract staging. The impact of the Revolution naturally affected all the theatres, which had either to find new plays by revolutionary writers or to produce the classics in a style accepted by the new spirit of the times. Tairov produced several of Eugene O'Neill's plays, using a formal style, no longer abstract, with settings designed in a naturalistic but simple fashion. The shapes and forms were severe, and usually monochromatic. While returning somewhat to the ideas of the Art Theatre, Tairov did not go so far as detailed naturalistic representation, and the actors were types rather than individuals, with their acting generalized rather than detailed in character. One of the best productions of the Kamerny Theatre was *The Optimistic Tragedy*, by Vishnevsky, which dealt with a detachment of sailors fighting in the Revolution. It deals with the War of the Revolution in the manner of an epic poem, and ends with the detachment being killed off one by one, not in despair but on a note of faith and confirmation of the ideas of the Revolution. The production was presented with clarity and strength, the actors played with sincerity and restraint, and the settings were expressive of the whole struggle. Such an idea, however, to be presented on the stage needed new forms to express it, new forms which were discovered by experimenting and by assessing new values to the setting, lighting, acting, music, and the various technical equipment of the theatre.

Vakhtangov, who died in 1922, at an early age, was a director who, though influenced by the Moscow Art Theatre, developed acting technique in a different direction. He saw the dangers in the exaggeration of characterization based on an inner personality, which might easily develop into a series of emotional experiences too psychological to be ' good

ABSTRACT PAINTERS FORSOOK NATURALISTIC
RENDERING OF OBJECTS AND SOUGHT AN
INTERESTING ARRANGEMENT OF SHAPE,
PATTERN, COLOUR, AND TEXTURE

theatre.' The actors of the Art Theatre built up their characterizations on their conception of the mind of the particular character, Vakhtangov's actors on their conception of the actions of the character. Vakhtangov's best-known production was *Princess Turandot*, a formal production using an abstract setting. His production methods, like Meyerhold's, made necessary the drastic editing or rewriting of the plays. After his death the Vakhtangov Theatre produced *Hamlet*, completely ignoring the philosophical side of the play and interpreting it as a struggle for the throne between heir and usurper.

What is so remarkable about the Russian theatres is that they withstood the impact of the First World War and the Revolution. Between 1914 and 1917 at the Art Theatre only three new plays were produced, owing to its difficulty in getting suitable works, as it refused to produce examples of reactionary drama. It continued giving performances of its repertoire of Chekhov, Gorky, and the classics. The young Soviet Government saw the educational value of the theatres, and gave them all the material help possible when necessary.

Stanislavsky and Dantchenko remained the directors of the Art Theatre, which had by now a second theatre and two music studios for producing opera and musical drama. The Art Theatre changed its name to the Moscow Gorky Theatre, but took some time to adjust itself to the needs of the Soviet. Several of its best actors had been touring in the country and were cut off by the fighting, so that it was not until about 1924 that the theatre recovered its old unity. By this time in addition to the older actors there were the youngsters who had grown up with the Revolution. The repertoire of classics was still retained, and gradually new plays were introduced. The policy of the supreme importance of the individual, which had been the Art Theatre's guiding star to fame in the past, had to be subjugated to political needs, to the portrayal of social justice and purpose. The production of *The Armoured Train*, by Ivanov, marked the final adjustment to the needs of the Soviet régime. In 1930 Tolstoy's *Resurrection* was an outstanding production of the Art Theatre. The play was about life in Tsarist Russia, and the most interesting feature of the production was the commentator, played by the great actor Katchalov, who stood in the orchestra and interpreted the author's and the theatre's views on the past. The productions of the Art Theatre were still realistic, but of a painted rather than a photographic realism. In the past the Art Theatre had kept out of politics, now it devoted certain productions to the political problems of the day. The actor remained the most important element in the productions, and his purpose was to disclose the philosophical idea underlying the play through the creation of great characters. During the revolutionary period of the theatre acting had to be simple and sincere, all subtlety was lost, and any false declamatory style would have been quite out of place.

Now that the period of revolution in the theatre, which manifested itself by the searching for new forms, the development of new technique, and the acquirement of new values, has passed, there have been established certain common principles in all Soviet theatres. Neither time nor expense is spared in the preparation of new plays or the fresh presentation of the classics. In every production the Soviet has accepted the Art Theatre's principle of complete unity of all the elements of the theatre, acting, scenery, lighting and technical equipment, and of the form that the production will take. This unity must express the idea of the play, whether it be of a philosophical or a social nature. Cubism, constructivism, or abstraction in any form has been rejected, whether it is present for a purely experimental or æsthetic reason or for its own sake. Throughout its history, in all branches of human effort, the Soviet Government has made great and courageous decisions when an experiment has proved of little value, either by entirely scrapping it, or possibly by moving in the opposite direction. It has seen the value of the theatre's period of experimentation, and it has now evolved a policy of theatrical naturalism, which is accepted solely because it is the most efficient vehicle of bringing the theatre, not to one particular section of the people, but to the entire masses.

How has this great period in the history of the theatre affected countries outside Russia? In Germany and America its influence was greatest, in England least of all. In Germany the idea of the director's iron discipline over the actors was already present in the company of the Duke of Meiningen, which played in Moscow towards the end of the nineteenth century, and from which Stanislavsky is said to have gained many of his ideas. But it is possibly

Max Reinhardt who has influenced the German theatre most. Reinhardt was already directing at the close of the nineteenth century, and was an extremely able organizer and administrator. He did not develop along the naturalistic path of Stanislavsky, but inaugurated a larger and more spectacular method of production. His theatre in Berlin, the Grosses Schauspielhaus, did not have the picture-frame stage of the Moscow Art Theatre, but was actually a converted

SETTING DESIGNED BY FERNAND LÉGER FOR A BALLET, SHOWING THE INFLUENCE
OF ABSTRACT PAINTING

circus building in which the arena was retained and merged with the stage by a series of rostrums. With lighting and well-developed stage machinery he built up dramatic effects, using crowds of actors in the arena, and bringing them among the audience. The stage was more often than not used as a background. Reinhardt's searching for form in a three-dimensional manner had not the effect of subduing the actors to the rôle of acrobats or mechanized portions of the setting, as had been the case in Meyerhold's theatre, but used them in a pageant sense of living drama. That Reinhardt's theatre produced the finest actors in Germany during the century is a tribute to his method of developing their part in his spectacular and dramatic productions. Religious subjects naturally suited this treatment, and he is remembered for his production in this country of *The Miracle*, a kind of modern morality play. He was forced to leave Germany when Hitler came to power, and he went to America, where he died in 1943, having established a dramatic school which will, no doubt, have some influence on the American theatre.

America was also fortunate in having the Moscow Art Theatre playing in the principal cities, when Dantchenko took the company there in 1925. The American theatre has, indeed, shown great vitality since the First World War. There are many reasons for this, perhaps the greatest being that in America the theatre is not an entirely middle-class institution, as in England. The American theatre has been a mirror of American life, and the diversity and richness of American life have been reflected in the theatre by plays dealing with vast and elemental problems. Plays have been written and produced on Broadway which deal with such subjects as the life of an engine-driver, two wandering tramps doing farm-work in California, the youth of Abraham Lincoln, a young Jewish violinist who becomes a prize-fighter, and

SURREALIST PAINTERS DELVED INTO THE SUB-
CONSCIOUS. THE NATURALISTIC RENDERING
OF A SERIES OF STRANGELY DISTORTED
OBJECTS AND FORMS PROVIDES A
WEIRD, DREAMLIKE ATMOSPHERE

life in the New York slums. The classics are presented in a variety of methods. Shakespeare remains the raw material for a producer to cut and trim according to his own æsthetic ideas. Thus in 1937 Orson Welles produced *Julius Cæsar*, representing the great Roman as a modern dictator. The stage was entirely devoid of scenery, and the setting was composed of a single rostrum. Change of scene was effected by lighting of various kinds, the spotlights being visible to the audience. The negroes have their own theatre, and have produced *Macbeth*, in which the scene is moved from Scotland to Haiti, and also such light operas as *The Mikado*, in which the music is pepped up to the momentum of swing. The American theatre was materially helped during the time of the great depression through the Works Progress Administration, and many new theatre projects were started under the Federal Government.

No less important are the little theatres, such as the Pasadena Community Playhouse and the Cleveland Playhouse. There are hundreds of these all over the States, some of which have municipal support, while others are completely independent. Most of them are well-founded and have their roots in the life of the community. They usually work on the repertory system—that is, one play produced each week or fortnight. Some have a permanent company of professional actors, while others use the talent of the community.

Another strong influence in the theatre world in America is the many theatre studios and workshops at the various universities and colleges. In America it is possible to take a degree in drama, and these workshops exist for purposes of experiment in production and setting, and the studying of the various techniques. In some cases the students have been encouraged to write plays set in their own environments, which have been produced at the college and subsequently have toured the state. The students have in turn left the university and gone out as teachers to high schools or elementary schools where the influence of their training is felt. Some graduates of college drama departments have gone into the professional theatre, where their influence has also been considerable.

What has happened in England on the stage? It would be a long story to trace back theatre history for the past forty years, but the main tendencies can be briefly described. First of all, the theatre, now a completely middle-class institution, including its writers, its actors, and most of its audience, has been disrupted, in common with the middle class, during this period of change and upheaval. Secondly, the theatre has not attracted the young male in any great numbers as it did in the past. A glance at the audience in any West End theatre will confirm that women are easily in the majority. At the present time the theatre has lost much of its vigour, although it is still very much alive. Technically, as always, it lags behind. One thing has been accepted, and that is the importance of the director. Now that technical equipment of the stage has been so developed that almost any effect of scenery or lighting can be obtained, it is necessary to have one person in charge to conceive the production as a unity. The lesson of the Moscow Art Theatre, that the actors must be submitted to a rigid discipline in order to obtain the director's unity of effect, has been applied only by a few directors, most of them allowing the actors considerable latitude. What has not been learnt is the care and attention necessary to production, by having rehearsals not for merely a fortnight or three weeks, as is usually the custom, but, as the Russians have done, for perhaps several months. Apart from some rare exceptions, the staging of plays has remained practically the same in this country, with very little change during a period of forty years. The popular West End success of this period has been almost invariably a realistic comedy of middle-class manners, usually with one setting for the entire three acts. As there was no scene-changing the settings have tended to become heavy and most realistic. Solid architectural detail has replaced the painted mouldings and panelling of earlier attempts at realism. The actors speak in conversational tones, as if they were in an actual drawing-room, and movement, the life-blood of drama, is at its lowest ebb.

Apart from the popular realistic comedy there have been some excellent productions of serious drama. In 1944 came the introduction of the true repertory system to the West End. Two companies developed a repertoire of four or five plays which were presented on different days of the week. The Old Vic Theatre Company at the New Theatre presented plays by Shakespeare, Shaw, Ibsen, and Chekhov, while at the Haymarket Theatre John Gielgud's company presented plays by Shakespeare, Congreve, John Webster, and Somerset Maugham. In the 1945 season the Old Vic continues as a repertory company.

Under the direction of John Burrell and the two leading actors, Ralph Richardson and Laurence Olivier, it is setting a standard in the production of serious drama unsurpassed in recent years. Plays are gradually added to their repertoire, and more time and care is thus possible in their production.

Further evidence of the demand for productions that break away from the popular realism of the West End is shown by the success of the numerous small intimate theatres that have been started in the last few years. Usually run as a club, in some cases with an extensive membership, they are ensured a permanent audience, and are able to produce unusual and interesting plays and half-forgotten classics. The Arts Theatre Club has had repertory seasons of English plays of various periods—Restoration, eighteenth-century, Victorian, as well as contemporary—and has played to full houses. The stages of these intimate theatres are usually poorly equipped, and ingenuity takes the place of elaborate machinery for scene-changing. There is developing a simple stylized type of production, which is based on naturalism, but is still theatrical. It offers much greater scope for the imaginative inter-pretation of a play, particularly of the classics, The spirit of a period is captured not by reproducing its sometimes tedious detail, but by simple generalizations. The stage becomes once again a platform, and no longer a drawing-room floor.

Many books have been written answering the question, " What's wrong with the theatre to-day? " and the answers variously given are: the commercialization of management—that is, that managers are no longer ex-actors with some taste or knowledge of the stage, but are just business-men—the fickleness of the public, the competition of the cinema, the dis-comfort of the outdated and badly designed theatres of the West End, the long run, and the dearth of good plays. Possibly all these reasons have some truth in them, although they seem strangely familiar, and there is a feeling that all this has been said before about the past theatres. When speaking of the theatre in this country we have so far referred only to the professional West End theatre of London. There are, of course, several repertory theatres in the provinces, which continue to flourish, if not to become wealthy. They have regular and faithful audiences, well trained in the important art of appreciating good plays, and by putting on good plays, not necessarily West End successes, they keep the theatre alive in the provinces.

In addition to the repertory theatres there are the numerous theatres and societies run by amateurs, which are flourishing all over the country, in village and town, and are linked together by the British Drama League. The standard of production varies, but usually it follows the professional theatre in style, except in certain rare cases such as the Unity Theatre, with its Living Newspaper and other experiments of a political nature. The British Drama League holds festivals at which various societies perform their plays in competition, and the drama festivals of Toynbee Hall, with its weekly programme of plays presented by various societies, also help greatly in encouraging self-criticism among the societies, with a corresponding raising of the standard of production.

The growth and popularity of amateur theatricals is also a measure of the general dissatis-faction with the professional theatre. When the professional theatre adapts itself to the changing social conditions, when it offers suitable fare to all classes, and when it becomes financially independent of the stall seats, then it will find new energy for further development.

It has first-rate actors, although the rank and file, because of the system of casting to type and long runs, are extremely limited in their range. It has some directors of taste and ability, and first-rate scenic designers and technicians. Two things are very badly wanted: plays written with some appreciation of the tremendous technical possibilities of the modern stage, and new and comfortable theatres in which every one has a good view of the stage. Finally, the theatre of to-day needs to look back at the past and see that the theatre has always been most successful when it has reflected the life of the people. The English theatre should be part of the national life of England, not the luxury of a certain class.

The Government had realized this fact in war-time, and under the Council for the Encouragement of Music and the Arts (C.E.M.A.) plays with professional casts were taken round the country, playing in small towns that normally had no theatre, and in factory canteens and Service camps. It is too soon to consider what the effect of the performance of these plays will have on people who have rarely if ever been inside a theatre, much less seen a play, but it is a fact that during the war, in spite of the Blitz, the theatre has boomed, and though the tendency is towards comedy and lighter entertainments, Shakespeare, Chekhov, Ibsen, and other classics have all seen production. Now in times of peace, under its new constitution as the Arts Council of Great Britain, it will continue to organize and develop this excellent service. It will also continue to aid financially productions by West End theatres of certain plays, and will give encouragement and assistance to amateur groups throughout the country. During the summer months many of the London parks have constructed open-air theatres, and plays, opera, and ballet have been performed, which, although subsidized by the London County Council, have independently been financially successful. It remains to be seen how municipal and State help in the theatre will develop in peace-time and what effect it will have on the theatre.

# APPENDIX I

## BOOK LIST

**Chapter I: The Greeks and the Romans**

ALLEN, J. T.: *Stage Antiquities of the Greeks and Romans and their Influence* (Harrap, 1927).

BIEBER, MARGARET: *The History of the Greek and Roman Theater* [1] (Oxford University Press, 1939).

HAIGH, A. E.: *The Attic Theatre* (Oxford University Press, 1907).

**Chapter II: The Middle Ages and the Renaissance**

CHAMBERS, SIR E. K.: *The Mediæval Stage* (Oxford University Press, 1903).

NICOLL, ALLARDYCE: *Masks, Mimes, and Miracles* [1] (Harrap, 1931).

**Chapter III: The Elizabethans**

CHAMBERS, SIR E. K.: *The Elizabethan Stage* (Oxford University Press, 1923).

LAWRENCE, W. J.: *The Physical Conditions of the Elizabethan Public Playhouse* (Oxford University Press, 1927).

PEARSON, HESKETH: *A Life of Shakespeare* (Penguin Books, 1942).

**Chapter IV: The Italian Comedians**

DUCHARTRE, PIERRE LOUIS (translated by R. T. WEAVER): *The Italian Comedy* [1] (Harrap, 1929).

NICOLL, ALLARDYCE: *Masks, Mimes, and Miracles* [1] (Harrap, 1931).

**Chapter V: The Restoration Theatre**

CAMPBELL, LILY B.: *Scenes and Machines on the English Stage during the Renaissance* (Cambridge University Press, 1923).

SUMMERS, MONTAGUE: *The Restoration Theatre* (Kegan Paul, 1934).

SUMMERS, MONTAGUE: *The Playhouse of Pepys* (Kegan Paul, 1935).

**Chapter VI: The Eighteenth Century**

CIBBER, COLLEY: *An Apology for his Life* (1740) (Dent).

THALER, ALWIN: *Shakespeare to Sheridan* (Milford, 1922).

**Chapter VII: The Victorians**

CRAIG, E. GORDON: *Henry Irving* (Dent, 1938).

WATSON, E. BRADLEE: *Sheridan to Robertson* (Oxford University Press, 1926).

**Chapter VIII: The Russians and Our Theatre**

CRAIG, E. GORDON: *The Theatre Advancing* (Constable, 1921).

CHARQUES, R. D.: *Footnotes to the Theatre* [1] (Peter Davies, 1938).

[1] Particularly well illustrated.

MACLEOD, JOSEPH: *The New Soviet Theatre* [1] (Allen and Unwin, 1943).

MARKOV, P. A.: *The Soviet Theatre* [1] (Gollancz, 1934).

NEMIROVITCH-DANTCHENKO, V.: *My Life in the Russian Theatre* (Geoffrey Bles, 1937).

VAN GYSEGHEM, ANDRÉ: *Theatre in Soviet Russia* [1] (Faber, 1943).

**All Chapters**

HUGHES, GLENN: *The Story of the Theatre* (Benn, 1929).

NICOLL, ALLARDYCE: *The Development of the Theatre* [1] (Harrap, 1937).

[1] Particularly well illustrated.

# APPENDIX II

## A List of Plays

The following list of plays is not intended as a catalogue of the classics,
but as a brief guide to some characteristic plays of the various periods.

### The Greeks

ÆSCHYLUS: *The Persians; The Oresteia* (a trilogy of *Agamemnon, Choephoræ,* and *The Eumenides*).
SOPHOCLES: *Ajax; Œdipus Tyrannus; Antigone.*
EURIPIDES: *Alcestis; Suppliants; Madness of Heracles; Electra.*
ARISTOPHANES: *The Acharnians; The Knights; The Clouds; The Peace; Lysistrata; The Birds.*

### The Romans

PLAUTUS: *Amphitruo; Epidicus; Truculentus.*
TERENCE: *Andria; Phormio; Adelphi.*
SENECA: *Agamemnon; Phædra; Thyestes.*

### The Middle Ages

MIRACLE PLAYS: *The Cornish Mystery Play of Mary Magdalene and the Apostles; The Cornish Mystery Play of the Three Maries; The Coventry Nativity Play; The Deluge; The Wakefield Miracle Play of the Crucifixion; The Wakefield Nativity Play.*
INTERLUDES: *The Four P's,* by John Heywood; *King Johan,* by John Bale; *Hycke Scorner.*
EARLY COMEDIES: *Ralph Roister Doister,* by Nicholas Udall; *Gammer Gurton's Needle,* by Mr S., Master of Arts (author unknown).
MORALITY: *Everyman.*

### The Elizabethans

JOHN LYLY: *Endimion; Campaspe.*
ROBERT GREENE: *James the Fourth; Friar Bacon and Friar Bungay.*
GEORGE PEELE: *David and Bethsabe.*
SACKVILLE AND NORTON: *Gorboduc.*
THOMAS KYD: *The Spanish Tragedy.*
CHRISTOPHER MARLOWE: *Tamburlaine; Dr Faustus.*
WILLIAM SHAKESPEARE: *Richard III; The Taming of the Shrew; Romeo and Juliet; A Midsummer Night's Dream; Richard II; The Merchant of Venice; Henry IV* (Parts I and II); *Henry V; The Merry Wives of Windsor; As You Like It; Julius Cæsar; Hamlet; Twelfth Night; Measure for Measure; Othello; King Lear; Macbeth; Antony and Cleopatra; Coriolanus; The Tempest.*
BEN JONSON: *Every Man in his Humour; The Alchemist; Volpone; Sejanus.*
BEAUMONT AND FLETCHER: *The Maid's Tragedy; Philaster; A King and No King; The Knight of the Burning Pestle.*
THOMAS DEKKER: *The Shoemaker's Holiday.*
JOHN MARSTON: *Antonio and Mellida.*
JOHN WEBSTER: *The White Devil; The Duchess of Malfi.*

### The Restoration

ELKANAH SETTLE: *The Empress of Morocco.*

WILLIAM DAVENANT: *The Siege of Rhodes; Love and Honour.*

JOHN DRYDEN: *The Conquest of Granada; All for Love; Sir Martin Mar-all; Marriage à la Mode; The Spanish Friar.*

THOMAS OTWAY: *Venice Preserved.*

WILLIAM CONGREVE: *The Mourning Bride; The Way of the World; Love for Love.*

GEORGE ETHEREGE: *The Man of Mode.*

WILLIAM WYCHERLEY: *The Gentleman Dancing Master; The Plain Dealer; The Country Wife.*

JOHN VANBRUGH: *The Relapse; The Confederacy.*

GEORGE FARQUHAR: *The Constant Couple; The Recruiting Officer; The Beaux' Stratagem.*

### Seventeenth-century French

PIERRE CORNEILLE: *Le Cid; Horace; Polyeucte.*

JEAN-BAPTISTE MOLIÈRE: *Tartuffe; Le Bourgeois Gentilhomme; Le Malade Imaginaire.*

JEAN RACINE: *Britannicus; Phèdre; Andromaque.*

### Eighteenth Century

JOHN GAY: *The Beggar's Opera.*

HENRY FIELDING: *Tom Thumb the Great.*

RICHARD STEELE: *The Conscious Lovers.*

JOSEPH ADDISON: *Cato.*

OLIVER GOLDSMITH: *She Stoops to Conquer.*

RICHARD BRINSLEY SHERIDAN: *The Rivals; The School for Scandal; Pizarro.*

### Eighteenth-century Italian

CARLO GOLDONI: *The Mistress of the Inn; The Liar.*

### Eighteenth-century French

PIERRE BEAUMARCHAIS: *The Barber of Seville.*

### Nineteenth Century

J. R. PLANCHÉ: *Success, or A Hit if You Like; The Merchant's Wedding.*

DOUGLAS JERROLD: *Black-ey'd Susan.*

T. E. WILKS: *The Ruby Ring, or The Murder at Sadler's Wells; Ben the Boatswain.*

DION BOUCICAULT: *London Assurance; The Corsican Brothers.*

TOM ROBERTSON: *Society; Caste; School; M.P.*

H. A. JONES: *The Silver King; The Liars.*

A. W. PINERO: *The Second Mrs Tanqueray; The Magistrate; Trelawney of the Wells.*

### Nineteenth-century European

HENRIK IBSEN (Norway): *Peer Gynt; Ghosts; Hedda Gabler; An Enemy of the People; The Master Builder; A Doll's House; The Wild Duck.*

AUGUST STRINDBERG (Sweden): *The Father; The Dance of Death.*

GERHART HAUPTMANN (Germany): *Before Sunrise; The Weavers.*

ANTON CHEKHOV (Russia): *The Bear; The Proposal; The Seagull; The Cherry Orchard; Uncle Vanya; The Wood Demon* [early version of *Uncle Vanya*]; *The Three Sisters.*

IVAN TURGENEV (Russia): *A Month in the Country.*

NIKOLAI GOGOL (Russia): *The Inspector-General.*
VICTOR HUGO (France): *Ruy Blas; Hernani.*

## Twentieth Century

OSCAR WILDE: *Lady Windermere's Fan; The Importance of Being Earnest; An Ideal Husband.*
GEORGE BERNARD SHAW: *Pygmalion; Candida; Heartbreak House; The Apple-cart; Geneva.*
J. M. BARRIE: *The Admirable Crichton; Dear Brutus; Mary Rose; Peter Pan.*
HARLEY GRANVILLE-BARKER: *The Voysey Inheritance.*
JOHN GALSWORTHY: *The Silver Box; Justice; Strife; The Skin Game; Escape.*
JOHN MASEFIELD: *The Tragedy of Nan; The Witch.*
JOHN DRINKWATER: *Abraham Lincoln; Oliver Cromwell.*
ST JOHN ERVINE: *The First Mrs Fraser; Robert's Wife.*
SOMERSET MAUGHAM: *A Man of Honour; Our Betters; East of Suez; The Letter; Sheppey.*
JAMES BRIDIE: *The Anatomist; The Last Trump; Tobias and the Angel.*
LORD DUNSANY: *A Night at an Inn.*
J. M. SYNGE: *Riders to the Sea; The Playboy of the Western World; The Shadow of the Glen.*
SEAN O'CASEY: *Juno and the Paycock; The Silver Tassie; The Plough and the Stars.*
NOEL COWARD: *Hay Fever; Private Lives; Blithe Spirit.*
EMLYN WILLIAMS: *Night Must Fall; The Corn is Green.*
DODIE SMITH: *Autumn Crocus; Dear Octopus.*
J. B. PRIESTLEY: *Dangerous Corner; Time and the Conways; Johnson over Jordan; They Came to a City; Desert Highway.*
T. S. ELIOT: *Murder in the Cathedral; Family Reunion.*
W. H. AUDEN and C. ISHERWOOD: *The Dog beneath the Skin; The Ascent of F6.*
STEPHEN SPENDER: *The Trial of a Judge.*
PAUL VINCENT CARROLL: *Shadow and Substance; The Old Foolishness; The White Steed; Things that are Cæsar's; The Strings, my Lord, are false.*
PETER USTINOV: *House of Regrets; The Banbury Nose.*

## Twentieth-century American

EUGENE O'NEILL: *The Emperor Jones; Anna Christie; Marco Millions; Mourning Becomes Electra; Desire under the Elms; Strange Interlude.*
ELMER RICE: *Street Scene; Counsellor-at-Law; Judgment Day.*
ROBERT SHERWOOD: *The Road to Rome; Idiot's Delight; There shall be no Night.*
CLIFFORD ODETS: *Waiting for Lefty; Golden Boy.*
MAXWELL ANDERSON: *Winterset; Saturday's Children.*
ROBERT ARDREY: *Thunder Rock; Casey Jones.*
THORNTON WILDER: *Our Town; The Skin of Our Teeth.*

## Twentieth-century European

MAURICE MAETERLINCK (Belgium): *The Blue Bird: The Death of Tintagiles.*
THE CAPEK BROTHERS (Czechoslovakia): *The Insect Play; R.U.R.* (by Karel Capek).
FERENCZ MOLNAR (Hungary): *Liliom.*
GARCIA LORCA (Spain): *Mariana; The Marriage of Blood.*
LUIGI PIRANDELLO (Italy): *Six Characters in Search of an Author.*

JEAN GIRAUDOUX (France): *Amphitryon 38; Judith.*

JULES ROMAINS (France): *M. Le Trouhadec in Monte Carlo; Knock.*

JEAN COCTEAU (France): *The Wedding on the Eiffel Tower; The Infernal Machine; Orphée.*

FRANÇOIS PORCHÉ (France): *Joan of Arc; Tsar Lenin.*

MAXIM GORKY (Russia): *The Lower Depths; Yegor Bulichoff; Dostigaeff and the Others.*

MICHAEL BULGAKOV (Russia): *The Days of the Turbins (The White Guard).*

LEONID ANDREYEV (Russia): *He who Gets Slapped.*

VALENTIN KATAEV (Russia): *Squaring the Circle.*

ALEXANDER AFINOGENEV (Russia): *Distant Point.*

KONSTANTIN SIMONOV (Russia): *The Russians.*

ALEXANDER OSTROVSKY (Russia): *Even a Wise Man Stumbles; Easy Money; Wolves and Sheep.*

# INDEX

# INDEX